*The Charlton Price Guide to*

# *ROYAL DOULTON BESWICK STORYBOOK FIGURINES*

*First Edition*

By
Jean Dale

Introduction
by
Louise Irvine

W. K. Cross
Publisher

The Charlton Press
Toronto, Ontario ✣ Birmingham, Michigan

Canadian Cataloguing In Publication Data
Main Entry under title:
The Charlton Price Guide to Royal Doulton Beswick Storybook Figurines
1994-
Biennial
ISSN 1198-1652
ISBN 0-88968- 130-9 (1st ed.)
1. Porcelain animals--Catalogs.
2. Royal Doulton figurines--Catalogues.
NK4660.C48 738.8'2'0294 C94-900402-2

**Printed in Canada**
**in the Province of Quebec**

*The Charlton Press*

**Editorial Office**
**2010 Yonge Street**
**Toronto, Canada. M4S 1Z9**
**Telephone (416) 488-4653 Fax: (416) 488-4656**

# EDITORIAL

| | |
|---|---|
| Editor | Jean Dale |
| Editorial Assistant | Davina Rowan |
| Layout | Frank van Lieshout |
| Photography | Marilyn and Peter Sweet |
| Advertising Manager | Donald Lorimer |

## ACKNOWLEDGEMENTS

The Charlton Press wishes to thank those who have helped with the First Edition of The Charlton Price Guide to Royal Doulton Beswick Storybook Figurines.

## SPECIAL THANKS

The publisher would like to thank Louise Irvine for writing the introduction to this First Edition. Louise is an independent writer and lecturer on Royal Doulton's history and products and is not connected with the pricing in this price guide. The photographs on inside chapter pages were kindly provided by Louise Irvine.
Our thanks also go to Royal Doulton (U.K.) Limited who helped with additional technical information, especially Valerie Baynton, Katharine Ellis and Julie McKeown.

## CONTRIBUTORS

Also the Publisher would like to thank the following individuals or companies who graciously supplied photographs or allowed us access to their collections for photographic purposed. We offer sincere thanks to:

Richard Dennis, Somerset, England; Mark Oliver, Phillips, London, England; Ed Pascoe, Pascoe and Co., Miami, Florida; Marilyn and Peter Sweet, Bolton, England; Leah Selig, Merrylands, Australia, Nick Tzimas, U. K. International Ceramics, Suffolk, England; Princess and Barry Weiss, New City, New York.

## A SPECIAL NOTE TO COLLECTORS

We welcome and appreciate any comments or suggestions in regard to the Charlton Price Guide to Royal Doulton Beswick Storybook Figurines. As with all first editions there will be errors and omissions. If they come to your attention please write informing us or if you would like to participate in pricing or supply previously unavailable data or information, please contact Jean Dale at (416) 488-4653.

# HOW TO USE THIS PRICE GUIDE

## THE PURPOSE

As with the other catalogues in Charlton's Royal Doulton reference and pricing library, this publication has been designed to serve two specific purposes. Its first purpose is to furnish the collector with accurate and detailed listings that provide the essential information needed to build a rewarding collection. Its second function is to provide collectors and dealers with current market prices for the complete line of Doulton and Beswick Storybook figures.

This catalogue covers the BEATRIX POTTER™, BRAMBLY HEDGE™, BUNNYKINS™ and THE SNOWMAN™ figures.

## STYLES AND VERSIONS

**STYLES:** A change in style occurs when a major element of the design is altered or modified as a result of a deliberate mould change. An example of this is *The Duchess With Flowers* (Style One) and *The Duchess With a Pie* Style Two).

**VERSIONS:** Versions are modifications in a minor style element such as the long ears becoming short ears on *Mr. Benjamin Bunny* and *Mr. Jeremy Fisher's* change in colourways from striped to spotted leggings.

Colourway variations are "version" changes as no major design element of the mould has been modified.

## THE LISTINGS

The Beatrix Potter figures are arranged alphabetically. At the beginning of the Beatrix Potter listings are three pages graphically outlining backstamp variations. Backstamps are illustrated for eight different varieties covering over fifty years of production. In the Beatrix Potter pricing charts the reader will see Beswick model and Doulton numbers, backstamp numbers and market prices.

The Brambly Hedge figures are listed by their DBH numbers. There are no backstamp variations known.

The Bunnykins figures are arranged in numerical order by DB numbers with the exception of the first six which were issued in the late '30's. These are *Billy, Farmer, Freddie, Mary, Mother* and *Reggie* and they are arranged alphabetically. There are seven different backstamps to the Bunnykins figures. Please see the section on backstamp variations at the beginning of the Bunnykins listings.

The Snowman series is listed in numerical order by the DS number. There are no backstamp variations.

All of the above listings include the modeller, where known, the name of the animal figure, designer, height, colour, date of issue, varieties and series.

## A WORD ON PRICING

The purpose of this catalogue is to give readers the most accurate, up-to-date retail prices for "Storybook" figures in the United States, Canada, the United Kingdom and Australia.

To accomplish this, The Charlton Press continues to access an international pricing panel of experts who submit prices based on both dealer and collector retail price activity as well as current auction results in the U. S., Canada, U. K. and Australia for the Bunnykins markets. These market prices are carefully averaged to reflect accurate valuations for figures in each of these markets. All discontinued figures are priced in this manner.

Current figures are priced according to the manufacturer's suggested retail price in each of the four market regions. Please be aware that price or promotional sales discounting is always possible and can result in lower prices than those listed.

The prices published herein are for figures in mint condition. Collectors are cautioned that a repaired or restored piece may be worth as little as 50 per cent of the value of the same figure in mint condition.

A further word on pricing. As mentioned previously, this is a catalogue giving prices for figures in the currency of a particular market (U.S. dollars for the American market and Sterling for the U.K. market.) The bulk of the prices given herein are not determined by currency exchange calculations but by actual market activity in the market concerned.

One exception, however, occurs in the case of current figures or recent limited editions issued in only one of the four markets. Since such items were priced by Doulton only in the country in which they were to be sold, prices for the other markets have been calculated using current currency exchange rates. These prices are noted with an asterisk.

Additionally, collectors must remember that all relevant information must be known to make a proper valuation of price. When comparing auction prices to catalogue prices, collectors and dealers must remember two important points. First, compare "apples and apples". Be sure that auction prices realized for figures include a buyer's premium if one is due. Buyer's premiums can range from 10% to 15% and on an expensive piece this amount can be substantial. Secondly, know whether a figure is restored, repaired or in mint condition. This fact may not be noted or explained in the listings and as a result, its price will not be reflective of that same piece in mint condition. Please be aware of repairs and restorations and the effect they may have on values.

A last word of caution. No pricing catalogue can be, or should be, a fixed price list. This catalogue must be considered a pricing guide only - showing the most current retail prices based on market demand within a particular region for the various figures.

## A NOTE ON THE INDEXES

At the back of this book the collector will find a total of nine indexes. While this may seem excessive, once you are familiar with the various indexes they will become very helpful.

First, there is a complete alphabetical index which lists all of the figures in this catalogue.

Then each of the four families of figures is given both an alphabetical and a numerical index cross-referencing the model or Doulton numbers. This will make light work of cross referencing your collection.

# TABLE OF CONTENTS

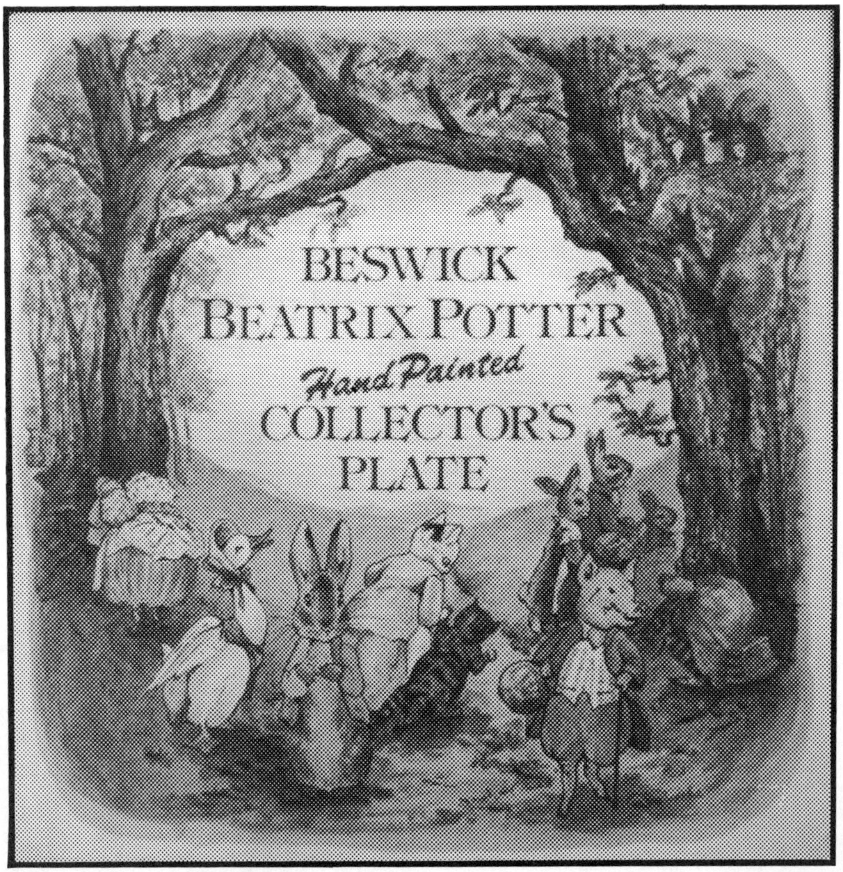
BESWICK
BEATRIX POTTER
Hand Painted
COLLECTOR'S
PLATE

# INTRODUCTION
## By Louise Irvine

**The History of Story Book Characters from the Royal Doulton, John Beswick and Royal Albert Studios.**

For over a century, the Royal Doulton Studios have entertained us with story book characters, particularly animals endowed with human personalities. In Victorian times, a group of frogs enacting a well-known fable raised a smile in much the same way as the antics of the BRAMBLY HEDGE™ mice amuse us today. The tales of BEATRIX POTTER™, with lots of different animals acting and conversing as if they were human, are as popular now as when they were first written in the early 1900s. Similarly the Bunnykins characters, first created in the 1930s, have survived the vagaries of fashion to become the most popular collectables of the 1990s. Obviously the idea of a creature simultaneously human and animal is deep rooted in our literary culture and it is interesting to trace when it first became apparent in the Doulton world.

**A Tinworth mouse group**

The Doulton factory was founded in London in 1815 but for the first 50 years production was confined to practical pottery. In the late 1860s, Sir Henry Doulton established an art studio, employing students from the Lambeth School of Art to decorate vases, jugs and plaques in fashionable Victorian styles. Some artists specialised in figurative sculpture, notably George Tinworth, who was the first to seek inspiration from well-known stories. The bible provided him with most of his subject matter but he also enjoyed reading the fables of Aesop and La Fontaine. These moralistic tales feature foxes, mice, lions and other creatures exemplifying human traits and they fascinated the Victorians, particularly after the publication of Darwin's theory of evolution. Tinworth modelled several fables groups in the 1880s, including *The Fox and the Ape, The Cat and the Cheese* and *The Ox and the Frogs*. Later he produced mice and frog subjects, based on his own observations of human nature, which reflect his perceptive sense of humor.

The potential for dressed-up animals to disguise a deeper message soon led to their widespread use in children's literature, notably *Alice's Adventures in Wonderland* and Lear's nonsense poems. In 1908, Kenneth Grahame wrote *Wind in the Willows* to comment on the behaviour of the English aristocracy but the exciting adventures of Mr. Toad subtly conceal the author's critical stance. The dapper toad in his pinstripes and tails was modelled shortly after his appearance by Lambeth artist Francis Pope and a companion piece shows Mr. Toad disguised as a washerwoman in order to escape from prison. Figures like these probably encouraged Beatrix Potter to approach the Lambeth studio in 1908 with a view to having her own animal characters immortalised in ceramic. Miss Potter has published several illustrated stories about her favourite animals since the success of *The Tale of Peter Rabbit*™ in 1902 and some characters had already appeared as cuddly toys and decorative motifs on clothes etc. Unfortunately an earlier contract with a German china firm made any arrangement with Doulton impossible but she tried on a later occasion to have figures made of her characters at

**Mr. Toad disguised as a washerwoman**

Grimwade's factory in Stoke-on-Trent. They suggested that Doulton's other factory in Burslem would be the best place to have the figures decorated but again plans fell through. It was not until after Miss Potter's death that her dream was realised when the John Beswick factory in Longton began making little figures inspired by her books.

The John Beswick factory was founded in 1894 to produce ornamental jugs, vases and other decorative fancies. By the 1940s the Beswick artists had established a reputation for quality animal modelling, particularly portraits of famous horses by Arthur Gredington. In 1947, Gredington demonstrated his versatility when he modelled *Jemima Puddleduck* at the suggestion of Lucy Beswick, the wife of the Managing Director. She had been inspired by a visit to Beatrix Potter's Lake District home where many of the tales are set. The success of this first study led to an initial collection of ten Beatrix Potter characters, including *Peter Rabbit, Benjamin Bunny* and *Mrs. Tiggy Winkle.*

Launched in 1948, the Beswick figures were welcomed with enthusiasm and the collection grew steadily throughout the 1950s and 60s. Gredington modelled sixteen more characters before handing over the responsibility to Albert Hallam in the late 1960s. As Head Mouldmaker, Hallam had produced many of the production moulds for the early Beatrix Potter characters so he was already familiar with the subject matter when he began modelling figures such as *Old Mr. Brown and Cecily Parsley.*

It was a time of transition for the company as Ewart Beswick was ready to retire but he had no heir for his successful business. Fortunately the Royal Doulton group was in the midst of an expansion programme and they acquired the Beswick factory in 1969. They soon benefitted from Beswick's expertise in the field of character animals as Albert Hallam began modelling little figures inspired by their famous BUNNYKINS™ nurseryware.

The Bunnykins characters were originally created in the 1930s by Barbara Vernon, a young nun who taught in an English convent school. She often entertained her pupils with sketches and stories about the Bunnykins characters and their potential as nurseryware decoration was recognised by her father, Cuthbert Bailey who was Doulton's Managing Director at the time. Bunnykins was launched in 1934 and, sixty years later, it is still one of the world's best selling nurseryware patterns.

There had been an attempt in 1939 to start a collection of Bunnykins figures but the Second World War intervened and production was not resumed, making the first six characters very rare indeed. Nine new style figures by Albert Hallam were launched in 1972, followed by three more the following year, and they were all derived from characters in the Bunnykins nurseryware scenes. When Albert Hallam retired in 1975, Graham Tongue became the Head Modeller at the Beswick Studio under Harry Sales, newly appointed as Design Manager.

Harry Sales was primarily a graphic artist and he dreamed up many new ideas for Bunnykins figures which Graham Tongue and others modelled during the 1980s. He created a new adult audience for Bunnykins with his witty sporting subjects, for example *Jogging Bunnykins* and *Bogey Bunnykins* and, as collector interest grew, he began to design special commissions such as *Uncle Sam* and *Collector Bunnykins.* At the same time, he was responsible for the continued development of the Beatrix Potter range, which was becoming increasingly difficult as the most popular characters had already been modelled. Favourites, such as Peter Rabbit and Jemima Puddleduck, were introduced in new poses and he came up with the idea of double figures, for example *Mr Benjamin Bunny and Peter Rabbit* and *Tabitha Twitchet and Miss Moppet.*

With their outstanding reputation for developing character animals in the Beatrix Potter and Bunnykins collections, it is not surprising that Royal Doulton artists were invited to work on the publishing sensation of the 1980s, the Brambly Hedge stories by Jill Barklem. Within three years of their launch the Spring, Summer, Autumn and Winter stories had been reprinted eleven times, translated into ten languages, and sold in excess of a million copies. Readers young and old were captivated by the enchanting world of the Brambly Hedge mice, as indeed was Harry Sales whose job it was to recreate the characters in the ceramic medium. In his own words "The first time I read the books and studied the illustrations I felt that I was experiencing something quite unique. Over a period of many years designing for the pottery industry one develops an awareness, a "feeling" for that something special. Brambly Hedge had this."

Ideas flowed quickly and eight leading characters were chosen from the seasonal stories for the initial collection, which was launched in 1983. Such was the response that they were soon joined by six more subjects, making a total of fourteen by 1986 when Harry left the company. Graham Tongue succeeded him as Design Manager and has continued to add new Brambly Hedge figures from the original stories on a regular basis. Miss Barklem's later titles *The Secret Staircase, The High Hills* and *The Sea Story,* have also provided inspiration for some of the more recent figures, for example *Mr and Mrs Saltapple* supply the Brambly Hedge community with salt in *The Sea Story.*

Encouraged by the amazing success of the Brambly Hedge collection, Royal Doulton's marketing executives were soon considering other new story book characters. Like millions of TV viewers, they were spell-bound by the magical film of *THE SNOWMAN™* which was first screened in 1982. Based on the illustrated book of the same name by Raymond Briggs, the animated film about a snowman who comes to life has become traditional Christmas entertainment in many parts of the world. The absence of words gives the tale a haunting quality and there is hardly a dry eye in the house when the little boy, James, awakes to find his Snowman friend has melted away after an exciting night exploring each other's worlds. Fortunately the Snowman lives on in more durable form in the Royal Doulton collection. Again Harry Sales was given the challenge of transforming this amorphous character into ceramic, whilst remaining faithful to Briggs' original soft crayon drawings. He succeeded in this difficult task by adding additional curves to the contours of the figures which gives them a like-like appearance. The first four figures were ready and approved by Raymond Briggs in 1985 and the collection grew steadily until 1990, latterly under the direction of Graham Tongue.

In the 1990s most of the Design Studio's resources have been concentrated on the Beatrix Potter and Bunnykins collections as there have been two major anniversaries to celebrate, the hundredth birthday of Peter Rabbit in 1993 and the Diamond Jubilee of Bunnykins in 1994. The collecting of Beatrix Potter and Bunnykins figures has reached epidemic proportions in the last couple of years, hence the need for this price guide, and no doubt their story book cousins, The Brambly Hedge mice and the Snowman characters, will grow in popularity as information becomes widespread.

### Collecting Beatrix Potter Figures

A number of factors have combined recently to make Beatrix Potter figures the 'hottest' collectables of the 1990s. The hundredth birthday of Peter Rabbit was celebrated amidst a storm of publicity in 1993 and the first reference book on the Beswick and Royal Albert figures was launched to coincide with all the celebrations. In addition, the centenary of the John Beswick factory this year has focused a lot of collector attention on their products.

The market has been stimulated by recent withdrawals from the range, twelve were announced at the end of 1993, making a total of twenty-four retired figures to date and six more are planned for the end of 1994. Prices are rocketing for the early discontinued figures and most collectors will need a bank loan to purchase *Duchess with Flowers*, the first Beatrix Potter figure to be retired, if indeed they are lucky enough to find one for sale.

**A group of Beatrix Potter books with the figures beside**

Ever since the Beswick factory launched their Beatrix Potter collection in 1948, most of the figures have been bought as gifts for children. However, many young fans have grown up to find they have some very valuable figures, with early modelling and backstamp variations, and collecting has begun in earnest to fill the gaps and find the rarities. Figures marked with a Beswick backstamp are most in demand as this trademark was replaced with the Royal Albert backstamp in 1989. The Royal Albert factory, another famous name in the Doulton group, produces all the Beatrix Potter tableware and the change of backstamps was made for distribution reasons. The most desirable Beswick marks are the gold varieties, which predate 1972, and these are often found on early modelling or colour variations, which also attract a premium price, for example *Mrs Rabbit* with her umbrella sticking out and *Mr Benjamin Bunny* with his pipe protruding.

As well as seeking out discontinued figures and rare variations, it is advisable to keep up to date with new models as they are introduced. A complete Beatrix Potter figure collection will encompass ninety-three of the standard size models, around three inches tall, and six large models, which are about twice the size. *Peter Rabbit*, the first of these large size models, was launched in 1993 with a special commemorative backstamp from the John Beswick studio and it changed in 1994 to the standard Royal Albert mark.

If owning all the Beatrix Potter figures is beyond the realms of possibility, whether for financial or display limitations, then why not focus on particular types of animals or characters from your favourite tales. There are twenty mice figures to find, a dozen cat characters and more than twenty rabbits, including six portraits of *Peter Rabbit* to date. There are also discontinued character jugs, relief modelled plaques and a ceramic display stand to look out for so happy hunting.

### Collecting Bunnykins Figures

The Diamond Jubilee of Bunnykins brings the famous rabbit family into the limelight once again and a special *60th Anniversary Bunnykins,* proudly carrying a birthday cake, is just one of ten new figures planned for 1994. This wide variety of introductions is indicative of today's tremendous enthusiasm for collecting Bunnykins. When the DB range was launched in 1972, most of the figures were purchased to amuse young children but the sporting characters of the 1980s began to appeal to adults and, in many cases, exchanging whimsical gifts developed into serious collecting.

***Artist Bunnykins*** **with the nurseryware plate which inspired the figure**

The Golden Jubilee celebrations in 1984 introduced Bunnykins to an even wider audience and led to the first collectors book, published by Richard Dennis. Fans were introduced to the entire range of nurseryware and figures, including the six large size models from 1939, which are extremely hard to find. Apart from these elusive models, it was relatively easy to form a complete collection of figures in the mid 1980s as the DB range consisted of just twenty-eight models with only four withdrawals. *Autumn Days, Springtime, The Artist* and *Grandpa's Story*, withdrawn in 1982 and 1983, are now very sought after on the secondary market but subsequent developments have generated much

**Harry Sales drawing for**
***Collector Bunnykins***

rarer characters. In 1986, Royal Doulton USA ordered new colourways of *Mr and Mrs Easter Bunnykins* to sell at a programme of artist demonstrations and these are now extremely difficult to find. Similarly, the two special colourways of *Bedtime Bunnykins,* made for D. H. Holmes and Belks department stores in 1987 and 1988, are now increasing in price as serious collectors try to get hold of them.

Although most Bunnykins characters are modelled with young children in mind, there have been several subjects exclusively for collectors, notably *Collector Bunnykins* which was commissioned by the International Collectors Club in 1987. As it was only offered for a six month period, it is now one of the rarest models in the DB range. *The Royal Doulton Collectors Band,* featuring the first limited edition Bunnykins figures, was launched at the London Doulton Fair in 1990, and since then there have been several limited pieces for exclusive distribution and special occasions. The overwhelming response to these special commissions was highlighted last year when the *Sergeant Mountie Bunnykins* sold out within hours of its launch at the Canadian Doulton show. Similarly, many of the limited editions commissioned by UK International Ceramics are now fully subscribed.

With this in mind, it is a good idea to buy the new Bunnykins figures as soon as they are issued. By the end of 1994, Royal Doulton will have allocated 150 DB numbers and, although a few intervening numbers have not been issued, notably *Ballet Bunnykins* DB 44, committed collectors now have quite a challenge to find them all. Figures are now regularly withdrawn from the range, adding to the excitement of the chase and, like many fellow collectors, you can always dream of finding all the rare 1939 models!

**Collecting Brambly Hedge Figures**

Since their introduction in 1983, the Brambly Hedge mice have overrun households in many parts of the world. They are scurrying about the shelves as Royal Doulton figures and even climbing up the wall on decorative plates. Far from being undesirable these particular mice are considered indispensable members of the family. Children frequently receive them as gifts from doting grandparents, but adults have also been seduced by the cosy timeless mouse world which Jill Barklem has created. The mood of rustic nostalgia has all been painstakingly researched. The interiors of the fieldmice homes are of the sort common in English farmhouses at the end of the 19th century and the food served is genuine country fare, based on old recipes and tasted in Jill Barklem's kitchen. The Brambly Hedge residents were all expertly drawn with the aid of her two mouse models, a keen understanding of zoology and a knowledge of historical costume.

The same attention to detail went into the Royal Doulton figures designed by Harry Sales. As he explains 'One important feature in the concept was that I chose poses which, when the figures are together, appear to be reacting to one another. I can imagine the fun children and the young at heart will have arranging the figures in conversational situations.' Essentially this sums up the collectability of the Brambly Hedge mice and the size of the series means they can all still be displayed effectively together on one shelf. To date there have been twenty four little figures and all are still relatively affordable, although the seven 1992 and 1993 withdrawals are beginning to have an impact on the secondary market. There is one unusual modelling variation to look out for as *Mr Toadflax's* tail was altered shortly after its introduction.

**Collecting Snowman Figures**

The seasonal appeal of The Snowman has tended to limit his collectability as most purchases are made around Christmas time and he is more popular in areas which regularly experience snow. Having said this, for some fans the wintry connotations are overshadowed by the inherent quality and humour of the models and there are keen collectors in sunny Florida as well as in Australia, where beach barbecues are typical Christmas celebrations.

Between 1985 and 1990, young children regularly received the new Snowman models in their Christmas stockings and the characters have been widely used as holiday decorations. Like the Brambly Hedge models, they were designed to interact and the little figure of *James,* gazing up in wonder can be positioned with various Snowman characters, whilst the band works very well as a separate display grouping. To date there are nineteen figures and two musical boxes to collect. More than half the range has been withdrawn and the discontinued models can now be quite difficult to locate. After a gap of four years, a new type of Snowman collectable was launched in July 1994, in the form of a miniature character jug by Martyn Alcock. Perhaps this will be the catalyst to a renewed interest in The Snowman collection.

### Making Story Book Characters

All the current story book characters are made at the John Beswick factory in Longton, which became part of the Royal Doulton group in 1969. They have over fifty years experience in the production of humorous figures and character animals and essentially the methods have not changed since the earliest days of the Beatrix Potter figures.

First of all the designer has to familiarise himself thoroughly with the character to be portrayed, reading the story and studying the illustration. Having chosen the most suitable pose for interpretation in ceramic, he will produce reference drawings for the modeller. Often he can only see one side of the character in the original illustration, so he has to improvise for his three dimensional model.

In consultation with the designer, the modeller will create the figure in modelling clay and, if satisfactory, a set of master moulds will be made in plaster of Paris. The number of mould parts will depend on the complexity of the figure and sometimes the head and arms have to be moulded separately. Two or three prototype figures will be cast from the master mould for colour trials and subsequent approval by the original artist or his agent.

In the case of the Beatrix Potter figures, all the models are scrutinised by the licensing agents, Copyrights, working on behalf of Miss Potter's original publishers Frederick Warne. Raymond Briggs, who was responsible for The Snowman, is generally quite relaxed about letting experts in other media interpret his drawings. He thought Royal Doulton's models were marvellous and really captured the spirit of the story although he maintained he would 'jolly well say so' if he thought they had got it wrong! Jill Barklem, the creator of Brambly Hedge, likes to get very involved in the licensing of her characters and Design Manager Harry Sales spent a lot of time working with her on the finer points of detail. Sometimes, slight modifications need to be made to the model or the colour scheme before the figure is approved by all concerned.

The next stage is to produce plaster of Paris working moulds from the master and supplies are sent to the casting department. An earthenware body is used to cast all the character figures produced at the John Beswick studio and it is poured into the mould in liquid form, known as slip. The moisture in the slip is absorbed into the plaster of Paris moulds and a 'skin' of clay forms the interior.

Once the clay has set to the required thickness, the excess clay is poured out and the mould is carefully dismantled. Any separate mould parts, such as projecting arms, will be joined on at this stage using slip as an adhesive and the seams will be gently sponged away. The figure is then allowed to dry slowly before it goes for its first firing. The high temperature in the kiln drives out the moisture in the body and the figure shrinks by about 1/12th of its original size, forming a hard 'biscuit' body.

Skilled decorators will paint the figure, using special under-glaze ceramic colours. They work from an approved colour sample and great care is taken to match the colours to the original book illustrations. A second firing hardens on the colour before the figure is coated with a solution of liquid glaze. When the figure is fired in the 'glost' kiln, it emerges with a shiny transparent finish which enhances and permanently protects the vibrant colours underneath. After a final inspection, the figures are despatched to china shops all over the world where they will capture the hearts of collectors young and old.

### Buying Current and Discontinued Story Book Characters

The Royal Doulton Company owns many well known china factories, including John Beswick, Royal Albert and Royal Doulton itself, and different trademarks are used for historical reasons or depending on the type of product. The Bunnykins, Brambly Hedge and Snowman collections feature the Royal Doulton backstamp, whilst the Beatrix Potter figures, originally part of the Beswick range, are now marked Royal Albert. All these varied collections are produced at the John Beswick factory in Longton, Stoke-on-Trent and models still being made at the factory today are referred to as 'current'. Most of the current story book figures can be purchased in specialist china shops or from mail order companies, specialising in collectables. However, some Bunnykins figures have been commissioned for exclusive distribution, notably the special editions for UK International Ceramics, and these are available direct from this company in the UK or from their appointed agents overseas.

Up to date information about new introductions to the story book collections is included in *Gallery* magazine, which is published quarterly by the Royal Doulton International Collectors Club. The Club regularly commissions exclusive collectables for its membership and Bunnykins figures have been featured in the past. Members also receive information about withdrawals to the collection in the various branch newsletters.

Once a piece has been withdrawn from production, it is referred to as 'discontinued' or 'retired' and it enters the secondary market. Many specialist Royal Doulton dealers around the world carry discontinued story book characters. Some have shops or showrooms but most sell by mail order and exhibit regularly at antique shows. Some of the more expensive Bunnykins and Beatrix Potter figures are now being sold at auction, for example *Duchess with Flowers* was included in a sale at Phillips of London in May 1994. Most story book characters do not yet qualify for the minimum lot price but it is still worth watching out for group lots at auctions or estate sales in case some of the character animals have been included. Perhaps a rare Beatrix Potter or Bunnykins colourway will not be recognised as such!

## WHERE TO BUY

Discontinued Storybook figures can be found in antique shops, markets and fair as well as auction houses. Specialist dealers in these figures attend many of the venues and events below.

### UNITED KINGDOM

#### Auction Houses

Phillips
101 New Bond Street
London W1

Christie's South Kensington
85 Old Brompton Road
London SW5

Bonhams
Montpelier Street
London SW7

Sotheby's
Summer's Plaace
Billingshurst, West Sussex

Louis Taylor
Percy Street
Hanley, Stoke-on-Trent

Peter Wilson
Victoria Gallery
Market Street
Nantwich, Cheshire

#### Antique Fairs

U.K. Doulton Collectors Fair
Park Lane Hotel
Piccadilly
London W1

Stafford International Doulton Fair
Stafford County Showground
Stafford

Doulton and Beswick Collectors Fair
National Motorcycle Museum
Meriden, Birmingham

#### Antique Markets

Portobello Road Market
London W11
Saturday only

New Caledonian Market
Bermondsey Square
London SE1
Friday morning

Alfie's Antique Market
13-25 Church Street
London NW8
Tuesday-Saturday

Camden Passage Market
(of Upper Street)
London N1
Wednesday and Saturday

### U.S.A.

#### Auction Houses

Phillips New York
406 East 79th Street
New York, NY 10021

#### Antique Fairs

Florida Doulton Convention
Sheraton Design Centre
Fort Lauderdale, Florida

Doulton Show
Sheraton Poste House
Cherry Hill, New Jersey

Doulton Show
Holiday Inn
Independence, Ohio

### CANADA

#### Auction Houses

D & J Ritchie Inc.
288 King Street East
Toronto, Ontario, M5A 1K4

#### Antique Shows

The Canadian Royal Doulton & Beswick Collectors Fair
Sheraton Toronto East Hotel
2035 Kennedy Road
Scarborough, Ontario

#### Antique Markets

Harbourfront Antique Market
390 Queen's Quay West
Toronto, Ontario
(Tuesday - Sunday)

### PLACES TO VISIT

John Beswick Factory Tour
Gold Street
Longton, Stoke-on-Trent
ST3 2JP
For opening times and tour information telephone
(0782) 292292

Royal Doulton Factory Tour
and Sir Henry Doulton Gallery
Nile Street
Burslem, Stoke-on-Trent
For opening times and tour information telephone
(0782) 744766

## CLUBS AND SOCIETIES

The Royal Doulton International Collectors Club was founded in 1980 to provide an information service on all aspects of the company's products, past and present. The Club's magazine "Gallery" is published four times a year and local branches also publish newsletters. There are also several regional groups in the U.S.A. which meet for lectures and other events and some publish newsletters. Contact the U.S.A. branch for further information.

**Headquarters and U.K. Branch**

Royal Doulton
Minton House
London Road
Stoke-on-Trent, ST4 7QD

**Australian Branch**

Royal Doulton Australia Pty Ltd.
17-23 Merriwa Street, Gordon
Australia, NSW 2072

**Canadian Branch**

Royal Doulton Canada Inc.
850 Progress Road
Scarborough, Ontario, M1H 3C4

**New Zealand Branch**

Royal Doulton
P.O. Box 2059
Auckland, New Zealand

**U.S.A. Branch**

Royal Doulton U.S.A. Inc
P.O. Box 1815
Somerset, New Jersey 08873

## FURTHER READING

### Storybook Figures

Royal Doulton Bunnykins Figures by Louise Irvine
Bunnykins Collectors Book by Louise Irvine
Beatrix Potter Figures edited by Louise Irvine
The Beswick Price Guide by Harvey May

### Animals, Figures and Character Jugs

Royal Doulton Figures by Desmond Eyles, Louise Irvine and Valerie Baynton
The Charlton Standard Catalogue of Royal Doulton Animals by Jean Dale
The Charlton Standard Catalogue of Royal Doulton Figurines by Jean Dale
The Charlton Standard Catalogue of Royal Doulton Jugs by Jean Dale
Collecting Character and Toby Jugs by Jocelyn Lukins
Collecting Doulton Animals by Jocelyn Lukins
Doulton Flambé Animals by Jocelyn Lukins
The Character Jug Collectors Handbook by Kevin Pearson
The Doulton Figure Collectors Handbook by Kevin Pearson

### General

Discovering Royal Doulton by Michael Doulton
The Doulton Story by Paul Atterbury and Louise Irvine
Royal Doulton Series Wares by Louise Irvine (Vols. 1-4)
Limited Edition Loving Cups and Jugs by Louise Irvine and Richard Dennis
Doulton for the Collector by Jocelyn Lukins
Doulton Kingsware Flasks by Jocelyn Lukins
Doulton Burslem Advertising Wares by Jocelyn Lukins
Doulton Lambeth Advertising Wares by Locelyn Lukins
The Doulton Lambeth Wares by Desmond Eyles
The Doulton Burslem Wares by Desmond Eyles
Hannah Barlow by Peter Rose
George Tinworth by Peter Rose
Sir Henry Doulton Biography by Edmund Gosse
Phillips Collectors Guide by Catherine Braithwaite
Royal Doulton by Jennifer Queree
Collecting Doulton Magazine Edited by Alan Blakeman, BBR Publishing

*BEATRIX POTTER*

# P

## Painting a portrait

## BEATRIX POTTER BACKSTAMPS

The backstamps of the Beatrix Potter figurines are currently divided into seven major catagories. These are listed below. For minor variations of these catagories please see the backstamp section in Louise Irvine's "Beatrix Potter Figures" published by U. K. International Ceramics.

### BP-1. BESWICK GOLD CIRCLE: 1948 -1954

Only one variety known. For cross reference see "Beatrix Potter Figures" backstamp G-1.

### BP-2. BESWICK GOLD OVAL: 1948-1972

There are six known varieties of this backstamp. For the minor varieties see "Beatrix Potter Figures" backstamps G-2 to G-7.

### BP-3. BESWICK BROWN LINE: 1972-1988

There are eight known varieties of this backstamp. For cross reference see "Beatrix Potter Figures" backstamps B1 to B8.

**Note:** A Gold Line backstamp has been reported. However until many more are reported it must be considered an oddity.

### BP-4. BESWICK DOULTON BROWN SCRIPT:

**1988-1989**

There are two known varieties of this backstamp. For cross reference see "Beatrix Potter Figures" backstamps B-9 to B-10.

## BP-5. ROYAL ALBERT GOLD CROWN: 1989

There are two known varieties of this backstamp, "with" and "without" the crown. For cross reference "see Beatrix Potter Figures" backstamp G-8.

## BP-6. ROYAL ALBERT BROWN CROWN: 1989 TO DATE

There are two known varieties of this backstamp "with" and "without" the crown. For cross reference see "Beatrix Potter Figures" backstamp B-11.

## BP-7. BESWICK BROWN OVAL: 1993 TO DATE.

One variation of this backstamp is the 100th Anniversary version of Peter Rabbit 1893-1993.

## AMIABLE GUINEA PIG™

| | |
|---|---|
| Modeller: | Albert Hallam |
| Height: | 3 1/2", 8.9 cm |
| Colour: | Tan jacket, white waistcoat, yellow trousers |
| Issued: | 1967 - 1983 |

BEATRIX POTTER'S
"Amiable Guinea-Pig
F. Warne & Co.Ltd.
Copyright
BESWICK ENGLAND

| *Back Stamp* | *Beswick Model* | *Doulton Number* | *U.S. $* | *Price Can. $* | *U. K. £* | *Aust. $* |
|---|---|---|---|---|---|---|
| BP-2 | 2061 | P2061 | 800.00 | 900.00 | 400.00 | 950.00 |
| BP-3 | | | 500.00 | 690.00 | 275.00 | 700.00 |

## AND THIS PIG HAD NONE™

| | |
|---|---|
| Modeller: | Martyn Alcock |
| Height: | 4 ', 10.1 cm |
| Colour: | Mauve dress, mottled burgundy and green shawl, brown hat |
| Issued: | 1992 to the present |

ROYAL ALBERT ®
ENGLAND
And this Pig had none
Beatrix Potter
© F. WARNE & CO. 1992
© 1992 ROYAL ALBERT LTD

| *Back Stamp* | *Beswick Model* | *Doulton Number* | *U.S. $* | *Price Can. $* | *U.K. £* | *Aust. $* |
|---|---|---|---|---|---|---|
| BP-6 | 3319 | P3319 | 29.95 | 49.95 | 13.50 | 57.00 |

## ANNA MARIA™

| | |
|---|---|
| Modeller: | Albert Hallam |
| Height: | 3", 7.6 cm |
| Colour: | Pale blue dress and white apron |
| Issued: | 1963 - 1983 |

BEATRIX POTTER'S
Anna Maria
F. WARNE & CO. LTD.
COPYRIGHT
BESWICK
ENGLAND

| *Back Stamp* | *Beswick Model* | *Doulton Number* | *U.S. $* | *Price Can. $* | *U.K. £* | *Aust. $* |
|---|---|---|---|---|---|---|
| BP-2 | 1851 | P1851 | 525.00 | 550.00 | 250.00 | 600.00 |
| BP-3 | | | 275.00 | 375.00 | 175.00 | 400.00 |

**APPLEY DAPPLY™**
**First Version (Bottle out)**

Modeller: Albert Hallam
Height: 3 1/4", 8.3 cm
Colour: Brown mouse, white apron blue trim. Blue bow. Yellow basket, tray of jam tarts
Issued: 1971 to 1980

| *Back Stamp* | *Beswick Model* | *Doulton Number* | *U.S. $* | *Price Can. $* | *U.K. £* | *Aust. $* |
|---|---|---|---|---|---|---|
| BP-2 | 2333 | P2333/1 | 225.00 | 225.00 | 100.00 | 250.00 |

**APPLEY DAPPLY™**
**Second Version (Bottle in)**

Modeller: Albert Hallam
Height: 3 1/4", 8.3 cm
Colour: Brown mouse, white apron blue trim. Blue bow. Yellow basket, tray of jam tarts
Issued: 1980 to the present

BEATRIX POTTER'S
"APPLEY DAPPLY"
F Warne & Co.Ltd
c Copyright 1971
BESWICK
ENGLAND

| *Back Stamp* | *Beswick Model* | *Doulton Number* | *U.S. $* | *Price Can. $* | *U.K. £* | *Aust. $* |
|---|---|---|---|---|---|---|
| BP-2 | 2333 | P2333/2 | 225.00 | 225.00 | 100.00 | 225.00 |
| BP-3 | | | 75.00 | 100.00 | 45.00 | 100.00 |
| BP-4 | | | 85.00 | 115.00 | 45.00 | 125.00 |
| BP-6 | | | 29.50 | 49.50 | 13.50 | 57.00 |

**AUNT PETTITOES™**

Modeller: Albert Hallam
Height: 3 3/4", 9.5 cm
Colour: Blue dress and white cap with blue polka dots
Issued: 1970 - 1993

BEATRIX POTTER'S
"Aunt Pettitoes"
F. Warne & Co.Ltd.
© Copyright 1970
BESWICK
ENGLAND

| *Back Stamp* | *Beswick Model* | *Doulton Number* | *U.S. $* | *Price Can. $* | *U.K. £* | *Aust.* |
|---|---|---|---|---|---|---|
| BP-2 | 2276 | P2276 | 325.00 | 250.00 | 100.00 | 275.00 |
| BP-3 | | | 75.00 | 90.00 | 45.00 | 100.00 |
| BP-4 | | | 85.00 | 115.00 | 45.00 | 125.00 |
| BP-6 | | | 45.00 | 50.00 | 15.00 | 75.00 |

**BABBITTY BUMBLE™**

Modeller: Warren Platt
Height: 2 3/4", 7.0 cm
Colour: Black and gold
Issued: 1989 - 1993

ROYAL ALBERT ®
ENGLAND
Babbitty Bumble
Beatrix Potter
© F. WARNE & CO. 1989
© 1989 ROYAL ALBERT LTD

| *Back Stamp* | *Beswick Model* | *Doulton Number* | *U.S. $* | *Price Can. $* | *U.K. £* | *Aust. $* |
|---|---|---|---|---|---|---|
| BP-6 | 2971 | P2971 | 55.00 | 50.00 | 25.00 | 57.00 |

**BENJAMIN ATE A LETTUCE LEAF™**

Modeller: Martyn Alcock
Height: 4 3/4", 11.9 cm
Colour: Brown and white and yellow
Issued: 1992 to the present

ROYAL ALBERT ®
ENGLAND
Benjemin ate a lettuce leaf
Beatrix Potter
© F. WARNE & CO. 1992
© 1992 ROYAL ALBERT LTD

| *Back Stamp* | *Beswick Model* | *Doulton Number* | *U.S. $* | *Price Can. $* | *U.K. £* | *Aust. $* |
|---|---|---|---|---|---|---|
| BP-6 | 3317 | P3317 | 29.95 | 49.95 | 13.50 | 57.00 |

**BENJAMIN BUNNY™**
**First Version (Ears out, Shoes out)**

Modeller: Arthur Gredington
Height: 4", 10.1 cm
Colour: Pale green jacket, light green beret with yellow and orange pom-pom
Issued: 1948 - 1974

BEATRIX POTTER'S
Benjamin Bunny
F. WARNE & Co. LTD
COPYRIGHT
BESWICK
ENGLAND

| *Back Stamp* | *Beswick Model* | *Doulton Number* | *U.S. $* | *Price Can. $* | *U.K. £* | *Aust. $* |
|---|---|---|---|---|---|---|
| BP-1 | 1105/1 | P1105/1 | 600.00 | 600.00 | 300.00 | 500.00 |
| BP-2 | | | 550.00 | 550.00 | 225.00 | 500.00 |
| BP-3 | | | 425.00 | 500.00 | 200.00 | 325.00 |

**BENJAMIN BUNNY™**
**Second Version (Ears out, Shoes in)**

Modeller: Arthur Gredington
Height: 4", 10.1 cm
Colour: Brown jacket, dark green beret with orange pom-pom
Issued: 1974 - c.1980

| *Back Stamp* | *Beswick Model* | *Doulton Number* | *U.S. $* | *Price Can. $* | *U.K. £* | *Aust. $* |
|---|---|---|---|---|---|---|
| BP-2 | 1105/2 | P1105/2 | 500.00 | 500.00 | 300.00 | 650.00 |
| BP-3 | | | 250.00 | 325.00 | 250.00 | 325.00 |

**BENJAMIN BUNNY™**
**Third Version (Ears in, Shoes in)**

Modeller: Arthur Gredington
Height: 4", 10.1 cm
Colour: Tan jacket, green beret with orange pom-pom
Issued: c.1980 to the present

| *Back Stamp* | *Beswick Model* | *Doulton Number* | *U.S. $* | *Price Can. $* | *U.K. £* | *Aust. $* |
|---|---|---|---|---|---|---|
| BP-3 | 1105/3 | P1105/3 | 60.00 | 75.00 | 65.00 | 80.00 |
| BP-4 | | | 65.00 | 85.00 | 65.00 | 90.00 |
| BP-5 | | | 75.00 | 100.00 | 50.00 | 100.00 |
| BP-6 | | | 29.95 | 49.50 | 13.50 | 57.00 |

**BENJAMIN BUNNY™**
**Fourth Version (Large)**

Modeller: Martyn Alcock
Height: 6 1/4", 15.9 cm
Size: Large
Colour: Tan jacket, Green beret with orange pom-pom
Issued: 1994

| *Back Stamp* | *Beswick Model* | *Doulton Number* | *U.S. $* | *Price Can. $* | *U.K.£* | *Aust. $* |
|---|---|---|---|---|---|---|
| BP-6 | 1105/4 | P1105/4 | 70.00 | 90.00 | 26.00 | 95.00 |

## BENJAMIN BUNNY SAT ON A BANK™
**First Version - Head looks down**

Modeller: David Lyttleton
Height: 3 3/4", 9.5 cm
Colour: Brown jacket
Issued: 1983 - 1988

BEATRIX POTTER'S
"Benjamin Bunny
"Sat on a bank"
© Frederick Warne P.L.C. 1983
BESWICK ENGLAND

| Back Stamp | Beswick Model | Doulton Number | U.S. $ | Price Can. $ | U.K. £ | Aust. $ |
|---|---|---|---|---|---|---|
| BP-3 | 2803/1 | P2803/1 | 125.00 | 150.00 | 95.00 | 150.00 |
| BP-4 | | | 175.00 | 200.00 | 75.00 | 200.00 |

## BENJAMIN BUNNY SAT ON A BANK™
**Second Version - Head looks up**

Modeller: David Lyttleton
Height: 3 3/4", 9.5 cm
Colour: Golden brown jacket
Issued: 1988 to the present

| Back Stamp | Beswick Model | Doulton Number | U.S. $ | Price Can. $ | U.K. £ | Aust. $ |
|---|---|---|---|---|---|---|
| BP-4 | 2803/2 | P2803/2 | 75.00 | 100.00 | 50.00 | 100.00 |
| BP-6 | | | 29.95 | 49.95 | 13.50 | 57.00 |

## BENJAMIN WAKES UP™

Modeller: Amanda Hughes-Lubeck
Height: 2 1/4", 5.7 cm
Colour: Green, white and orange
Issued: 1991 to the present

ROYAL ALBERT ®
ENGLAND
Benjamin Wakes Up
Beatrix Potter
© F. WARNE & CO. 1990
© 1990 ROYAL ALBERT LTD

| Back Stamp | Beswick Model | Doulton Number | U.S. $ | Price Can. $ | U.K. £ | Aust. $ |
|---|---|---|---|---|---|---|
| BP-6 | 3234 | P3234 | 29.95 | 49.95 | 13.50 | 57.00 |

**CECILY PARSLEY™**
**First Version (Head Down)**

| | |
|---|---|
| Modeller: | Arthur Gredington |
| Height: | 4", 10.1 cm |
| Colour: | Blue dress, white apron, brown pail |
| Issued: | 1965 - 1979 |

| Back Stamp | Beswick Model | Doulton Number | U.S. $ | Price Can. $ | U.K. £ | Aust. $ |
|---|---|---|---|---|---|---|
| BP-2 | 1941/1 | P1941/1 | 325.00 | 175.00 | 75.00 | 150.00 |
| BP-3 | | | 85.00 | 100.00 | 45.00 | 100.00 |

**CECILY PARSLEY™**
**Second Version (Head Up)**

| | |
|---|---|
| Modeller: | Arthur Gredington |
| Height: | 4", 10.1 cm |
| Colour: | Blue dress, white apron |
| Issued: | 1979 - 1993 |

| Back Stamp | Beswick Model | Doulton Number | U.S. $ | Price Can. $ | U.K. £ | Aust. $ |
|---|---|---|---|---|---|---|
| BP-3 | 1941/2 | P1941/2 | 75.00 | 100.00 | 45.00 | 75.00 |
| BP-4 | | | 75.00 | 100.00 | 45.00 | 85.00 |
| BP-6 | | | 30.00 | 50.00 | 25.00 | 65.00 |

**CHIPPY HACKEE™**

| | |
|---|---|
| Modeller: | David Lyttleton |
| Height: | 3 3/4" |
| Colour: | Pale green blanket, white handkerchief, green foot bath |
| Issued: | 1979 - 1993 |

| Back Stamp | Beswick Model | Doulton Number | U.S. $ | Price Can. $ | U.K. £ | Aust. $ |
|---|---|---|---|---|---|---|
| BP-3 | 2627 | P2627 | 85.00 | 115.00 | 50.00 | 115.00 |
| BP-4 | | | 100.00 | 150.00 | 50.00 | 150.00 |
| BP-6 | | | 40.00 | 40.00 | 20.00 | 57.00 |

## CHRISTMAS STOCKING™

Modeller: Martyn Alcock
Height: 3 1/4", 8.3 cm
Colour: Brown mice, red and white striped stocking
Issued: 1991 - 1994

ROYAL ALBERT ®
ENGLAND
The Christmas Stocking
Beatrix Potter
© F. WARNE & CO. 1991
© 1991 ROYAL ALBERT LTD

| Back Stamp | Beswick Model | Doulton Number | U.S. $ | Price Can. $ | U.K. £ | Aust. $ |
|---|---|---|---|---|---|---|
| BP-6 | 3257 | P3257 | 65.00 | 95.00 | 25.00 | 70.00 |

## COTTONTAIL™

Modeller: David Lyttleton
Height: 3 3/4", 9.5 cm
Colour: Blue dress, brown chair
Issued: 1985 to the present

ROYAL ALBERT ®
ENGLAND
Cottontail
Beatrix Potter

| Back Stamp | Beswick Model | Doulton Number | U.S. $ | Price Can. $ | U.K.£ | Aust. $ |
|---|---|---|---|---|---|---|
| BP-3 | 2878 | P2878 | 60.00 | 75.00 | 40.00 | 75.00 |
| BP-4 | | | 75.00 | 100.00 | 40.00 | 100.00 |
| BP-6 | | | 29.95 | 49.95 | 13.50 | 55.00 |

## COUSIN RIBBY™

Modeller: Albert Hallam
Height: 3 1/2", 8.9 cm
Colour: Pink skirt and hat, green apron, blue shawl, yellow basket
Issued: 1970 - 1993

BEATRIX POTTER'S
"Cousin Ribby"
F. Warne & Co.Ltd.
© Copyright 1970
BESWICK ENGLAND

| Back Stamp | Beswick Model | Doulton Number | U.S. $ | Price Can. $ | U.K. £ | Aust. $ |
|---|---|---|---|---|---|---|
| BP-2 | 2284 | P2284 | 250.00 | 300.00 | 125.00 | 300.00 |
| BP-3 | | | 65.00 | 90.00 | 45.00 | 90.00 |
| BP-4 | | | 75.00 | 100.00 | 35.00 | 100.00 |
| BP-6 | | | 30.00 | 50.00 | 20.00 | 60.00 |

### DIGGORY DIGGORY DELVET™

Modeller: David Lyttleton
Height: 2 3/4", 7 cm
Colour: Grey mole
Issued: 1982 to the present

BEATRIX POTTER'S
Diggory Diggory Delvet
© Frederick Warne P.L.C. 1982
BESWICK ENGLAND

| *Back Stamp* | *Beswick Model* | *Doulton Number* | *U.S. $* | *Price Can. $* | *U.K. £* | *Aust. $* |
|---|---|---|---|---|---|---|
| BP-3 | 2713 | P2713 | 70.00 | 100.00 | 45.00 | 100.00 |
| BP-4 | | | 85.00 | 125.00 | 50.00 | 135.00 |
| BP-6 | | | 29.95 | 49.95 | 13.50 | 70.00 |

### DISPLAY STAND™

Modeller: Andrew Brindley
Height: 12 1/2" x 12 1/2", 31.7 cm x 31.7 cm
Colour: Brown, light brown
Issued: 1970 to the present

| *Back Stamp* | *Beswick Model* | *Doulton Number* | *U.S. $* | *Price Can. $* | *U.K. £* | *Aust. $* |
|---|---|---|---|---|---|---|
| Beswick | 2295 | P2295 | 150.00 | 200.00 | 95.00 | 200.00 |
| Doulton | | | 50.00 | 175.00 | 40.00 | 90.00 |

### DUCHESS™
**Style One (Holding Flowers)**

Modeller: Graham Orwell
Height: 3 3/4", 9.5 cm
Colour: Black dog holding bunch of flowers
Issued: 1955 - 1967

| *Back Stamp* | *Beswick Model* | *Doulton Number* | *U.S. $* | *Price Can. $* | *U.K. £* | *Aust. $* |
|---|---|---|---|---|---|---|
| BP-2 | 1355 | P1355 | | Exremely Rare | | |

Realized at Philips Doulton Auction, London, May 25, 1994 , £1,870.00 including commissions.

## DUCHESS™
**Style Two (Holding a Pie)**

Modeller: Graham Tongue
Height: 4", 10.1 cm
Colour: Black dog, blue bow, light brown pie
Issued: 1979-1982

BEATRIX POTTER'S
"Duchess"
F. Warne & Co.Ltd.
© Copyright 1979
BESWICK ENGLAND

| *Back Stamp* | *Beswick Model* | *Doulton Number* | *U.S. $* | *Price Can. $* | *U.K. £* | *Aust. $* |
|---|---|---|---|---|---|---|
| BP-3 | 2601 | P2601 | 225.00 | 250.00 | 110.00 | 200.00 |

## FIERCE BAD RABBIT™
**First Version (Feet out)**

Modeller: David Lyttleton
Height: 4 3/4", 12.1 cm
Colour: Brown and white rabbit, red-brown carrot, green seat
Issued: 1977 to 1980

BEATRIX POTTER'S
"Fierce Bad Rabbit"
F. Warne & Co.Ltd.
© Copyright 1977
BESWICK ENGLAND

| *Back Stamp* | *Beswick Model* | *Doulton Number* | *U.S. $* | *Price Can. $* | *U.K. £* | *Aust. $* |
|---|---|---|---|---|---|---|
| BP-3 | 2586 | P2586/1 | 225.00 | 350.00 | 145.00 | 350.00 |

## FIERCE BAD RABBIT™
**Second Version (Feet in)**

Modeller: David Lyttleton
Height: 4 3/4", 12.1 cm
Colour: Brown and white rabbit, red-brown carrot, green seat
Issued: 1980 to the present

| *Back Stamp* | *Beswick Model* | *Doulton Number* | *U.S. $* | *Price Can. $* | *U.K. £* | *Aust. $* |
|---|---|---|---|---|---|---|
| BP-3 | 2586 | P2586 | 70.00 | 100.00 | 45.00 | 100.00 |
| BP-4 | | | 75.00 | 125.00 | 45.00 | 125.00 |
| BP-6 | | | 29.95 | 49.50 | 13.50 | 70.00 |

## FLOPSY, MOPSY AND COTTONTAIL™

Modeller: Arthur Gredington
Height: 2 1/2", 6.4 cm
Colour: Brown and white rabbits wearing rose-pink cloaks
Issued: 1954 to the present

BEATRIX POTTER'S
Flopsy Mopsy and Cottontail"
F. Warne & Co. Ltd.
©, Copyright 1954
BESWICK ENGLAND

| *Back Stamp* | *Beswick Model* | *Doulton Number* | *U.S. $* | *Price Can. $* | *U.K. £* | *Aust. $* |
|---|---|---|---|---|---|---|
| BP-2 | 1274 | P1274 | 350.00 | 200.00 | 95.00 | 200.00 |
| BP-3 | | | 70.00 | 80.00 | 45.00 | 80.00 |
| BP-4 | | | 75.00 | 90.00 | 40.00 | 90.00 |
| BP-5 | | | 100.00 | 100.00 | 15.00 | 100.00 |
| BP-6 | | | 29.95 | 49.95 | 13.50 | 60.00 |

## FOXY READING COUNTRY NEWS™

Modeller: Amanda Hughes-Lubeck
Height: 4 1/4", 10.8 cm
Colour: Brown and green
Issued: 1990 to the present

ROYAL ALBERT ®
ENGLAND
Foxy Reading
Beatrix Potter
© F. WARNE & CO. 1990
© 1990 ROYAL ALBERT LTD

| *Back Stamp* | *Beswick Model* | *Doulton Number* | *U.S. $* | *Price Can. $* | *U.K. £* | *Aust. $* |
|---|---|---|---|---|---|---|
| BP-6 | 3219 | P3219 | 55.00 | 69.50 | 21.00 | 91.00 |

## FOXY WHISKERED GENTLEMAN™

Modeller: Arthur Gredington
Height: 4 3/4", 12.1 cm
Colour: Pale green jacket and trousers, pink waistcoat
Issued: 1954 to the present

BEATRIX POTTER'S
Foxy Whiskered Gentleman
BESWICK ENGLAND
F. Warne & Co. Ltd.
Copyright

| *Back Stamp* | *Beswick Model* | *Doulton Number* | *U.S. $* | *Price Can. $* | *U.K. £* | *Aust. $* |
|---|---|---|---|---|---|---|
| BP-2 | 1277 | P1277 | 300.00 | 350.00 | 125.00 | 350.00 |
| BP-3 | | | 65.00 | 125.00 | 60.00 | 125.00 |
| BP-4 | | | 75.00 | 125.00 | 60.00 | 140.00 |
| BP-6 | | | 29.95 | 49.50 | 13.50 | 57.00 |

## GENTLEMAN MOUSE MADE A BOW™

Modeller: Ted Chawner
Height: 3", 7.6 cm
Colour: Brown, blue and white
Issued: 1990 to the present

ROYAL ALBERT ®
ENGLAND
Gentleman Mouse
Made a Bow
Beatrix Potter
© F. WARNE & CO. 19[illegible]
© 1988 ROYAL ALBERT LTD

| Back Stamp | Beswick Model | Doulton Number | U.S. $ | Price Can. $ | U.K. £ | Aust. $ |
|---|---|---|---|---|---|---|
| BP-6 | 3200 | P3200 | 29.95 | 49.95 | 13.50 | 64.00 |

## GINGER™

Modeller: David Lyttleton
Height: 3 3/4", 9.5 cm
Colour: Green, white and brown
Issued: 1976 - 1982

BEATRIX POTTER'S
"Ginger"
F. Warne & Co.Ltd.
© Copyright 1976
BESWICK ENGLAND

| Back Stamp | Beswick Model | Doulton Number | U.S. $ | Price Can. $ | U.K. £ | Aust. $ |
|---|---|---|---|---|---|---|
| BP-3 | 2559 | P2559 | 850.00 | 1,100.00 | 500.00 | 1,200.00 |

## GOODY TIPTOES™

Modeller: Arthur Gredington
Height: 3 1/2", 8.9 cm
Colour: Grey squirrel wearing pink dress and white apron, brown sack with yellow nuts
Issued: 1961 to the present

BEATRIX POTTER'S
"Goody Tiptoes"
F. Warne & Co.Ltd.
© Copyright 1961
BESWICK
ENGLAND

| Back Stamp | Beswick Model | Doulton Number | U.S. $ | Price Can. $ | U.K. £ | Aust. $ |
|---|---|---|---|---|---|---|
| BP-2 | 1675 | P1675 | 275.00 | 300.00 | 95.00 | 325.00 |
| BP-3 | | | 65.00 | 80.00 | 40.00 | 90.00 |
| BP-4 | | | 75.00 | 95.00 | 45.00 | 110.00 |
| BP-6 | | | 29.95 | 49.95 | 13.50 | 64.00 |

## GOODY AND TIMMY TIPTOES™

Modeller: David Lyttleton
Height: 4", 10.1 cm
Colour: Timmy: Rose coat
Goody: Pink overdress with green and biege underskirt, green umbrella
Issued: 1986 to the present

ROYAL ALBERT ®
ENGLAND
Goody and Timmy Tiptoes
Beatrix Potter
© F WARNE & CO 1986
© 1989 ROYAL ALBERT LTD

| Back Stamp | Beswick Model | Doulton Number | Price U.S. $ | Can. $ | U.K. £ | Aust. $ |
|---|---|---|---|---|---|---|
| BP-3 | 2957 | P2957 | 275.00 | 300.00 | 150.00 | 300.00 |
| BP-4 | | | 325.00 | 375.00 | 150.00 | 350.00 |
| BP-6 | | | 55.00 | 75.00 | 24.00 | 85.00 |

## HUNCA MUNCA™

Modeller: Arthur Gredington
Height: 2 3/4", 7 cm
Colour: Blue dress, white apron, pink blanket and straw cradle
Issued: 1951 to the present

BESWICK ENGLAND
BEATRIX POTTER'S
"HUNCA MUNCA"
F. WARNE & CO. LTD.
COPYRIGHT

| Back Stamp | Beswick Model | Doulton Number | Price U.S. $ | Can. $ | U.K. £ | Aust. $ |
|---|---|---|---|---|---|---|
| BP-1 | 1198 | P1198 | 295.00 | 350.00 | 125.00 | 375.00 |
| BP-2 | | | 250.00 | 300.00 | 100.00 | 325.00 |
| BP-3 | | | 65.00 | 100.00 | 65.00 | 110.00 |
| BP-4 | | | 75.00 | 125.00 | 60.00 | 135.00 |
| BP-5 | | | 100.00 | 100.00 | 50.00 | 125.00 |
| BP-6 | | | 29.95 | 49.95 | 13.50 | 57.00 |

## HUNCA MUNCA SPILLS THE BEADS™

Modeller: Martyn Alcock
Height: 3 1/4", 8.3 cm
Colour: Brown mouse, blue and white rice jar
Issued: 1992 to the present

ROYAL ALBERT ®
ENGLAND
Hunca Munca spills the beads
Beatrix Potter
© F WARNE & CO 1991
© 1992 ROYAL ALBERT LTD

| Back Stamp | Beswick Model | Doulton Number | Price U.S. $ | Can. $ | U.K. £ | Aust. $ |
|---|---|---|---|---|---|---|
| BP-6 | 3288 | P3288 | 34.00 | 49.95 | 15.95 | 62.00 |

## HUNCA MUNCA SWEEPING™

Modeller: David Lyttleton
Height: 3 1/2", 8.9 cm
Colour: Mauve patterned dress with white apron, green broom handle
Issued: 1977 to the present

BEATRIX POTTER'S
Hunca Munca Sweeping
F Warne & Co.Ltd.
© Copyright 1977
BESWICK ENGLAND

| *Back Stamp* | *Beswick Model* | *Doulton Number* | *U.S. $* | *Price Can. $* | *U.K. £* | *Aust. $* |
|---|---|---|---|---|---|---|
| BP-3 | 2584 | P2584 | 65.00 | 130.00 | 65.00 | 150.00 |
| BP-4 | | | 75.00 | 150.00 | 75.00 | 175.00 |
| BP-6 | | | 29.95 | 49.95 | 13.50 | 57.00 |

BEATRIX POTTER'S
Jemima Puddleduck
F. Warne & Co. Ltd.
Copyright
BESWICK
ENGLAND

## JEMIMA PUDDLE-DUCK™
**First Version**

Modeller: Arthur Gredington
Height: 4 3/4", 12.1cm
Colour: White duck, mauve shawl, light blue bonnet
Issued: 1948 to the present

| *Back Stamp* | *Beswick Model* | *Doulton Number* | *U.S. $* | *Price Can. $* | *U.K. £* | *Aust. $* |
|---|---|---|---|---|---|---|
| BP-1 | 1092/1 | P1092/1 | 275.00 | 325.00 | 125.00 | 350.00 |
| BP-2 | | | 225.00 | 250.00 | 100.00 | 300.00 |
| BP-3 | | | 65.00 | 90.00 | 65.00 | 100.00 |
| BP-4 | | | 75.00 | 100.00 | 45.00 | 115.00 |
| BP-5 | | | 100.00 | 125.00 | 50.00 | 135.00 |
| BP-6 | | | 29.95 | 49.50 | 13.50 | 64.00 |

## JEMIMA PUDDLE-DUCK™
**Second Version (Large Size)**

Modeller: Arthur Gredington
Height: 6", 15 cm
Size: Large
Colour: White duck, mauve shawl light blue bonnet
Issued: 1994

| *Back Stamp* | *Beswick Model* | *Doulton Number* | *U.S. $* | *Price Can. $* | *U.K. £* | *Aust. $* |
|---|---|---|---|---|---|---|
| BP-6 | 1092/2 | P1092/2 | 65.00 | 88.00 | 25.95 | 98.00 |
| BP-7 | | | 65.00 | 88.00 | 25.95 | 98.00 |

### JEMIMA PUDDLE-DUCK CHARACTER JUG™

Modeller: Ted Chawner
Height: 4", 10.1 cm
Colour: Blue, pink and white
Issued: 1989 - 1992

BEATRIX POTTER
'Jemima Puddle-Duck'
© F. Warne & Co. 1988
Licensed by Copyrights
Studio of Royal Doulton
England

| Back Stamp | Beswick Model | Doulton Number | U.S. $ | Price Can. $ | U.K. £ | Aust. $ |
|---|---|---|---|---|---|---|
| BP-4 | | | 150.00 | 225.00 | 100.00 | 90.00 |
| BP-6 | | | 115.00 | 135.00 | 65.00 | 90.00 |

### JEMIMA PUDDLE-DUCK AND FOXY WHISKERED GENTLEMAN™

Modeller: Ted Chawner
Height: 4 3/4", 12.1 cm
Colour: Brown, green, white and blue
Issued: 1990 to the present

ROYAL ALBERT ®
ENGLAND
Jemima Puddleduck with
Foxy Whiskered Gentleman
Beatrix Potter
© F WARNE & CO 1989
© 1989 ROYAL ALBERT LTD

| Back Stamp | Beswick Model | Doulton Number | U.S. $ | Price Can. $ | U.K. £ | Aust. $ |
|---|---|---|---|---|---|---|
| BP- | 3193 | P3193 | 80.00 | 100.00 | 24.00 | 91.00 |

### JEMIMA PUDDLE-DUCK AND FOXY WHISKERED GENTLEMAN PLAQUE™

Modeller: Harry Sales and David Lyttleton
Height: 7 1/2" x 7 1/2", 19.1 cm x 19.1 cm
Colour: Brown, green, white and blue
Issued: 1977 - 1982

| Back Stamp | Beswick Model | Doulton Number | U.S. $ | Price Can. $ | U.K. £ | Aust. S |
|---|---|---|---|---|---|---|
| BP-3 | 2594 | P2594 | 175.00 | 200.00 | 75.00 | 225.00 |

## JEMIMA PUDDLEDUCK MADE A FEATHER NEST™

| | |
|---|---|
| Modeller: | David Lyttleton |
| Height: | 2 1/4", 5.7 cm |
| Colour: | Blue hat, mauve and green shawl and white duck |
| Issued: | 1983 to the present |

BEATRIX POTTER'S
Jemima Puddleduck
Made a feather nest
© Frederick Warne P.L.C. 1983
BESWICK
ENGLAND

| Back Stamp | Beswick Model | Doulton Number | U.S. $ | Price Can. $ | U.K. £ | Aust. $ |
|---|---|---|---|---|---|---|
| BP-3 | 2823 | P2823 | 65.00 | 80.00 | 40.00 | 100.00 |
| BP-4 | | | 75.00 | 100.00 | 40.00 | 115.00 |
| BP-6 | | | 29.95 | 0.00 | 13.50 | 57.00 |

## JEMIMA PUDDLE-DUCK PLAQUE™

| | |
|---|---|
| Modeller: | Albert Hallam |
| Height: | 6", 15.2 cm |
| Colour: | White duck, mauve shawl |
| Issued: | 1967 - 1969 |

| Back Stamp | Beswick Model | Doulton Number | U.S. $ | Price Can. $ | U.K. £ | Aust. $ |
|---|---|---|---|---|---|---|
| BP-2 | 2082 | P2082 | | Extremely Rare | | |

*Photograph Not Available at Press Time*

## JOHN JOINER™

| | |
|---|---|
| Modeller: | Graham Tongue |
| Height: | 2 1/2", 6.4 cm |
| Colour: | Brown dog wearing green jacket |
| Issued: | 1990 to the present |

ROYAL ALBERT ®
ENGLAND
John Joiner
Beatrix Potter
© F. WARNE & CO. 1990
© 1990 ROYAL ALBERT LTD

| Back Stamp | Beswick Model | Doulton Number | U.S. $ | Price Can. $ | U.K. £ | Aust. $ |
|---|---|---|---|---|---|---|
| BP-6 | 2965 | P2965 | 29.95 | 49.95 | 13.50 | 65.00 |

## JOHNNY TOWN-MOUSE™

Modeller: Arthur Gredington
Height: 3 1/2", 8.9 cm
Colour: Pale blue jacket, white and brown waistcoat
Issued: 1954 - 1993

| *Back Stamp* | *Beswick Model* | *Doulton Number* | *U.S. $* | *Price Can. $* | *U.K. £* | *Aust. $* |
|---|---|---|---|---|---|---|
| BP-1 | 1276 | P1276 | 275.00 | 350.00 | 125.00 | 400.00 |
| BP-2 | | | 225.00 | 250.00 | 95.00 | 275.00 |
| BP-3 | | | 65.00 | 90.00 | 45.00 | 110.00 |
| BP-4 | | | 75.00 | 100.00 | 45.00 | 125.00 |
| BP-6 | | | 30.00 | 50.00 | 15.00 | 57.00 |

## JOHNNY TOWN-MOUSE WITH BAG™

Modeller: Ted Chawner
Height: 3 1/2", 8.9 cm
Colour: Light brown coat and hat, yellow/cream waistcoat
Issued: 1988 - 1994

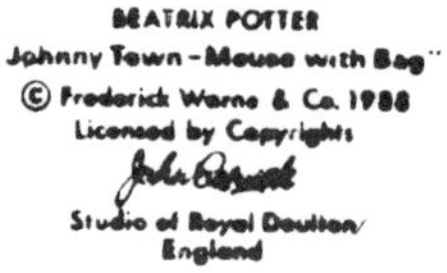


| *Back Stamp* | *Beswick Model* | *Doulton Number* | *U.S. $* | *Price Can. $* | *U.K. £* | *Aust. $* |
|---|---|---|---|---|---|---|
| BP-4 | 3094 | P3094 | 250.00 | 375.00 | 195.00 | 400.00 |
| BP-6 | | | 50.00 | 75.00 | 17.95 | 70.00 |

## LADY MOUSE™

Modeller: Arthur Gredington
Height: 4", 10.1 cm
Colour: White dress with yellow trim and blue polka dot sleeves, white hat with purple and blue highlights
Issued: 1950 to the present

| *Back Stamp* | *Beswick Model* | *Doulton Number* | *U.S. $* | *Price Can. $* | *U.K. £* | *Aust. $* |
|---|---|---|---|---|---|---|
| BP-2 | 1183 | P1183 | 275.00 | 300.00 | 110.00 | 375.00 |
| BP-3 | | | 75.00 | 180.00 | 55.00 | 125.00 |
| BP-4 | | | 85.00 | 125.00 | 55.00 | 140.00 |
| BP-6 | | | 29.95 | 49.95 | 13.50 | 64.00 |

## LADY MOUSE MADE A CURTSEY™

Modeller: Amanda Hughes-Lubeck
Height: 3 1/4", 8.3 cm
Colour: Purple-pink and white
Issued: 1990 to the present

ROYAL ALBERT ®
ENGLAND
Lady Mouse made a Curtsy
Beatrix Potter
© F. WARNE & CO. 1990
© 1990 ROYAL ALBERT LTD

| *Back Stamp* | *Beswick Model* | *Doulton Number* | *U.S. $* | *Price Can. $* | *U.K. £* | *Aust. $* |
|---|---|---|---|---|---|---|
| BP-6 | 3220 | P3220 | 29.95 | 49.95 | 13.50 | 57.00 |

## LITTLE BLACK RABBIT™

Modeller: David Lyttleton
Height: 4 1/2", 11.4 cm
Colour: Black rabbit wearing green waistcoat
Issued: 1977 to the present

BEATRIX POTTER'S
"Little Black Rabbit"
F. Warne & Co.Ltd.
© Copyright 1977
BESWICK ENGLAND

| *Back Stamp* | *Beswick Model* | *Doulton Number* | *U.S. $* | *Price Can. $* | *U.K. £* | *Aust. $* |
|---|---|---|---|---|---|---|
| BP-3 | 2585 | P2585 | 65.00 | 90.00 | 50.00 | 100.00 |
| BP-4 | | | 75.00 | 115.00 | 50.00 | 125.00 |
| BP-6 | | | 29.95 | 49.95 | 13.50 | 85.00 |

## LITTLE PIG ROBINSON™
**First Version (Blue Stripes)**

Modeller: Arthur Gredington
Height: 4", 10.2 cm
Colour: White and blue striped dress; brown basket with yellow cauliflowers
Issued: 1948 - c.1970

BEATRIX POTTER'S
Little Pig Robinson
F. WARNE & Co. Ltd. COPYRIGHT
BESWICK ENGLAND

| *Back Stamp* | *Beswick Model* | *Doulton Number* | *U.S. $* | *Price Can. $* | *U.K. £* | *Aust. $* |
|---|---|---|---|---|---|---|
| BP-2 | 1104/1 | P1104/1 | 500.00 | 550.00 | 225.00 | 550.00 |

## LITTLE PIG ROBINSON™
**Second Version (Blue Checked)**

| | |
|---|---|
| Modeller: | Arthur Gredington |
| Height: | 3 1/2", 8.9 cm |
| Colour: | Blue dress, brown basket with cream cauliflowers |
| Issued: | c.1970 to the present |

BEATRIX POTTER'S
"Little Pig Robinson"
F. Warne & Co.Ltd.
© Copyright 1948
BESWICK
ENGLAND

| *Back Stamp* | *Beswick Model* | *Doulton Number* | *U.S. $* | *Price Can. $* | *U.K. £* | *Aust. $* |
|---|---|---|---|---|---|---|
| BP-2 | 1104/2 | P1104/2 | | | Rare | |
| BP-3 | | | 75.00 | 110.00 | 45.00 | 115.00 |
| BP-4 | | | 85.00 | 125.00 | 45.00 | 130.00 |
| BP-6 | | | 30.00 | 49.95 | 13.50 | 67.00 |

## LITTLE PIG ROBINSON SPYING™

| | |
|---|---|
| Modeller: | Ted Chawner |
| Height: | 3 1/2", 8.9 cm |
| Colour: | Blue and white striped dress, rose-pink chair |
| Issued: | 1987 - 1993 |

BEATRIX POTTER
"Little Pig Robinson
Spying"
© Frederick Warne & Co. 1987
Licensed by Copyrights
BESWICK ENGLAND

| *Back Stamp* | *Beswick Model* | *Doulton Number* | *U.S. $* | *Price Can. $* | *U.K. £* | *Aust. $* |
|---|---|---|---|---|---|---|
| BP-3 | 3031 | P3031 | 250.00 | 350.00 | 175.00 | 350.00 |
| BP-4 | | | 275.00 | 350.00 | 175.00 | 350.00 |
| BP-6 | | | 100.00 | 100.00 | 35.00 | 90.00 |

## MISS DORMOUSE™

| | |
|---|---|
| Modeller: | Martyn Alcock |
| Height: | 4", 10.1 cm |
| Colour: | Blue, white and pink |
| Issued: | 1991 to the present |

ROYAL ALBERT ®
ENGLAND
Miss Dormouse
Beatrix Potter
© F. WARNE & CO. 1991
© 1991 ROYAL ALBERT LTD

| *Back Stamp* | *Beswick Model* | *Doulton Number* | *U.S. $* | *Price Can. $* | *U.K. £* | *Aust. $* |
|---|---|---|---|---|---|---|
| BP-6 | 3251 | P3251 | 65.00 | 95.00 | 19.95 | 57.00 |

## MISS MOPPET™

**First Version (Mottled Brown Cat)**

Modeller: Arthur Gredington
Height: 3", 7.6 cm
Colour: Dark brown cat, blue checkered kerchief
Issued: 1954 - c.1978

BEATRIX POTTER'S
"Miss. Moppet
F. Warne & Co.Ltd.
© Copyright 1954
BESWICK ENGLAND

| Back Stamp | Beswick Model | Doulton Number | U.S. $ | Price Can. $ | U.K. £ | Aust. $ |
|---|---|---|---|---|---|---|
| BP-2 | 1275 | P1275A | 225.00 | 275.00 | 95.00 | 300.00 |
| BP-3 | | | 200.00 | 250.00 | 80.00 | 275.00 |

## MISS MOPPET™

**Second Version (Brown Striped Cat)**

Modeller: Arthur Gredington
Height: 3", 7.6 cm
Colour: Light brown cat, blue checkered kerchief
Issued: 1954 to the present

BEATRIX POTTER'S
"Miss. Moppet
F. Warne & Co.Ltd.
© Copyright 1954
BESWICK ENGLAND

| Back Stamp | Beswick Model | Doulton Number | U.S. $ | Price Can. $ | U.K. £ | Aust. $ |
|---|---|---|---|---|---|---|
| BP-3 | 1275 | P1275B | 65.00 | 100.00 | 45.00 | 110.00 |
| BP-4 | | | 75.00 | 115.00 | 45.00 | 115.00 |
| BP-6 | | | 29.95 | 49.95 | 13.50 | 57.00 |

## MITTENS AND MOPPET™

Modeller: Ted Chawner
Height: 3 3/4", 9.5 cm
Colour: Blue, brown and grey
Issued: 1990 - 1994

ROYAL ALBERT
ENGLAND
Mittens and Moppet
Beatrix Potter
© F. WARNE & CO. 19[illegible]
© 19[illegible] ROYAL ALBERT LTD

| Back Stamp | Beswick Model | Doulton Number | U.S. $ | Price Can. $ | U.K. £ | Aust. $ |
|---|---|---|---|---|---|---|
| BP-6 | 3197 | P3197 | 50.00 | 75.00 | 19.95 | 80.00 |

## MOTHER LADYBIRD™

Modeller: Warren Platt
Height: 2 1/2", 6 .4 cm
Colour: Red and black
Issued: 1989 to the present

ROYAL ALBERT®
ENGLAND
Mother Ladybird
Beatrix Potter
© F. WARNE & CO. 1989
© 1989 ROYAL ALBERT LTD

| *Back Stamp* | *Beswick Model* | *Doulton Number* | *U.S. $* | *Price Can. $* | *U.K. £* | *Aust. $* |
|---|---|---|---|---|---|---|
| BP-6 | 2966 | P2966 | 34.00 | 55.00 | 13.50 | 57.00 |

## MR. ALDERMAN PTOLEMY™

Modeller: Graham Tongue
Height: 3 1/2", 8.9 cm
Colour: Brown, grey and green
Issued: 1973 to the present

BEATRIX POTTER'S
"Mr. Alderman Ptolemy
F. Warne & Co. Ltd.
© Copyright 1973
BESWICK
MADE IN ENGLAND

| *Back Stamp* | *Beswick Model* | *Doulton Number* | *U.S. $* | *Price Can. $* | *U.K. £* | *Aust. $* |
|---|---|---|---|---|---|---|
| BP-3 | 2424 | P2424 | 85.00 | 200.00 | 100.00 | 225.00 |
| BP-4 | | | 95.00 | 200.00 | 100.00 | 225.00 |
| BP-6 | | | 29.95 | 49.95 | 13.50 | 64.00 |

## MR. BENJAMIN BUNNY™
**First Version (Pipe Out)**

Modeller: Arthur Gredington
Height: 4 1/4", 10.8 cm
Colour: Dark maroon jacket, yellow waistcoat;
Issued: 1965 - 1974

BEATRIX POTTER'S
"Mr. Benjamin Bunny
F. Warne & Co.Ltd.
© Copyright 1965
BESWICK ENGLAND

| *Back Stamp* | *Beswick Model* | *Doulton Number* | *U.S. $* | *Price Can. $* | *U.K. £* | *Aust. $* |
|---|---|---|---|---|---|---|
| BP-2 | 1940/1 | P1940/1 | 600.00 | 750.00 | 300.00 | 800.00 |
| BP-3 | | | 500.00 | 650.00 | 275.00 | 700.00 |

**MR. BENJAMIN BUNNY™**
**Second Version (Pipe In)**

Modeller: Arthur Gredington
Height: 4 1/2", 11.4 cm
Colour: Lilac jacket, yellow waistcoat
Issued: 1974 to the present

BEATRIX POTTER
"Mr. Benjamin Bunny"
© F. Warne & Co. 1965
Licensed by Copyrights
BESWICK ENGLAND

| *Back Stamp* | *Beswick Model* | *Doulton Number* | *U.S. $* | *Price Can. $* | *U.K. £* | *Aust. $* |
|---|---|---|---|---|---|---|
| BP-3 | 1940/2 | P1940/2 | 65.00 | 85.00 | 40.00 | 85.00 |
| BP-4 | | | 75.00 | 85.00 | 40.00 | 100.00 |
| BP-5 | | | 100.00 | 100.00 | 50.00 | 100.00 |
| BP-6 | | | 29.95 | 49.95 | 13.50 | 62.00 |

**MR. BENJAMIN BUNNY AND PETER RABBIT™**

Modeller: Alan Maslankowski
Height: 4", 10.1 cm
Colour: Benjamin Bunny: Lilac jacket yellow waistcoat; Peter Rabbit: blue jacket
Issued: 1975 to the present

BEATRIX POTTER'S
Mr. Benjamin Bunny
& Peter Rabbit
F. Warne & Co.Ltd.
© Copyright 1975
BESWICK ENGLAND

| *Back Stamp* | *Beswick Model* | *Doulton Number* | *U.S. $* | *Price Can. $* | *U.K. £* | *Aust. $* |
|---|---|---|---|---|---|---|
| BP-3 | 2509 | P2509 | 200.00 | 250.00 | 85.00 | 275.00 |
| BP-4 | | | 225.00 | 275.00 | 95.00 | 300.00 |
| BP-6 | | | 50.00 | 69.95 | 19.95 | 91.00 |

**MR. DRAKE PUDDLE-DUCK™**

Modeller: David Lyttleton
Height: 4", 10.1 cm
Colour: White duck, blue waistcoat and trousers
Issued: 1979 to the present

BEATRIX POTTER
"Mr. Drake Puddle-Duck"
© Frederick Warne & Co. 1979
Licensed by Copyrights
BESWICK ENGLAND

| *Back Stamp* | *Beswick Model* | *Doulton Number* | *U.S. $* | *Price Can. $* | *U.K. £* | *Aust. $* |
|---|---|---|---|---|---|---|
| BP-3 | 2628 | P2628 | 65.00 | 95.00 | 55.00 | 100.00 |
| BP-4 | | | 75.00 | 110.00 | 65.00 | 115.00 |
| BP-6 | | | 29.95 | 49.95 | 13.50 | 64.00 |

## MR. JACKSON™
**First Version (Green Frog)**

Modeller: Albert Hallam
Height: 2 3/4", 7.0 cm
Colour: Green frog wearing mauve jacket
Issued: 1974 - c.1980

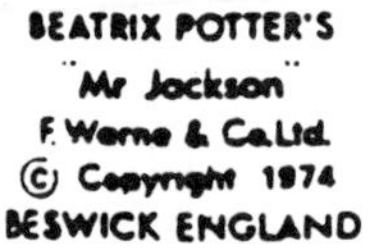

| Back Stamp | Beswick Model | Doulton Number | Price U.S. $ | Can. $ | U.K. £ | Aust. $ |
|---|---|---|---|---|---|---|
| BP-3 | 2453/1 | P2453/1 | 450.00 | 500.00 | 250.00 | 550.00 |

## MR. JACKSON™
**Second Version (Brown Frog)**

Modeller: Albert Hallam
Height: 2 3/4", 7.0 cm
Colour: Brown frog wearing mauve jacket
Issued: 1980 to the present

| Back Stamp | Beswick Model | Doulton Number | Price U.S. $ | Can. $ | U.K. £ | Aust. $ |
|---|---|---|---|---|---|---|
| BP-3 | 2453/2 | P2453/2 | 65.00 | 130.00 | 65.00 | 140.00 |
| BP-4 | | | 75.00 | 130.00 | 65.00 | 140.00 |
| BP-6 | | | 29.95 | 49.95 | 13.50 | 70.00 |

## MR. JEREMY FISHER™
**First Version (Spotted Legs)**

Modeller: Arthur Gredington
Height: 3", 7.6 cm
Colour: Lilac coat, green frog with small brown spots on head and legs
Issued: 1950 - c.1980

| Back Stamp | Beswick Model | Doulton Number | Price U.S. $ | Can. $ | U.K. £ | Aust. $ |
|---|---|---|---|---|---|---|
| BP-2 | 1157/1 | P1157/1 | 325.00 | 350.00 | 160.00 | 375.00 |
| BP-3 | | | 200.00 | 250.00 | 95.00 | 275.00 |

**MR. JEREMY FISHER™**
**Second Version (Striped Legs)**

Modeller: Arthur Gredington
Height: 3", 7.6 cm
Colour: Lilac coat, green frog with large spots on head and stripes on legs
Issued: c.1980 to the present

BEATRIX POTTER
"Jeremy Fisher"
© Frederick Warne & Co. 1950
Licensed by Copyrights
BESWICK ENGLAND

| *Back Stamp* | *Beswick Model* | *Doulton Number* | *U.S. $* | *Price Can. $* | *U.K. £* | *Aust. $* |
|---|---|---|---|---|---|---|
| BP-3 | 1157/2 | P1157/2 | 75.00 | 110.00 | 45.00 | 125.00 |
| BP-4 | | | 85.00 | 125.00 | 45.00 | 140.00 |
| BP-6 | | | 29.95 | 49.95 | 13.50 | 64.00 |

**MR. JEREMY FISHER™**
**Third Version (Large Size)**

Modeller: Martyn Alcock
Height: 5", 12.7 cm
Size: Large
Colour: Lilac coat, green frog
Issued: 1994

| *Back Stamp* | *Beswick Model* | *Doulton Number* | *U.S. $* | *Price Can. $* | *U.K. £* | *Aust. $* |
|---|---|---|---|---|---|---|
| BP-6 | | | 65.00 | 88.00 | 25.95 | 98.00 |

**MR. JEREMY FISHER CHARACTER JUG™**

Modeller: Graham Tongue
Height: 3", 7.6 cm
Colour: Mauve
Issued: 1987 - 1992

John Beswick
ENGLAND
BEATRIX POTTER
"Jeremy Fisher"
© 1987 Frederick Warne & Co.
Licensed by Copyrights

| *Back Stamp* | *Beswick Model* | *Doulton Number* | *U.S. $* | *Price Can. $* | *U.K. £* | *Aust. $* |
|---|---|---|---|---|---|---|
| BP-4 | | | 135.00 | 150.00 | 65.00 | 80.00 |
| BP-6 | | | 115.00 | 49.95 | 13.50 | 80.00 |

## MR. JEREMY FISHER DIGGING™

Modeller: Ted Chawner
Height: 3 3/4", 9.5 cm
Colour: Mauve coat, pink waistcoat, white cravat, green frog, with brown highlights
Issued: 1986 - 1994

| *Back Stamp* | *Beswick Model* | *Doulton Number* | *U.S. $* | *Price Can. $* | *U.K. £* | *Aust. $* |
|---|---|---|---|---|---|---|
| BP-3 | 3090 | P3090 | 250.00 | 350.00 | 195.00 | 375.00 |
| BP-4 | | | 275.00 | 400.00 | 195.00 | 425.00 |
| BP-6 | | | 50.00 | 75.00 | 17.95 | 70.00 |

## MR. TOD™

Modeller: Ted Chawner
Height: 4 3/4", 12.1 cm
Colour: Green suit, red waistcoat, dark brown walking stick
Issued: 1988 - 1993

| *Back Stamp* | *Beswick Model* | *Doulton Number* | *U.S. $* | *Price Can. $* | *U.K. £* | *Aust. $* |
|---|---|---|---|---|---|---|
| BP-4 | 3091 | P3091 | 275.00 | 400.00 | 200.00 | 350.00 |
| BP-6 | | | 95.00 | 135.00 | 35.00 | 125.00 |

## MRS. FLOPSY BUNNY™

Modeller: Arthur Gredington
Height: 4", 10.1 cm
Colour: Light blue dress, pink bag
Issued: 1965 to the present

| *Back Stamp* | *Beswick Model* | *Doulton Number* | *U.S. $* | *Price Can. $* | *U.K. £* | *Aust. $* |
|---|---|---|---|---|---|---|
| BP-2 | 1942 | P1942 | 225.00 | 225.00 | 95.00 | 250.00 |
| BP-3 | | | 65.00 | 90.00 | 45.00 | 100.00 |
| BP-4 | | | 75.00 | 115.00 | 45.00 | 125.00 |
| BP-6 | | | 29.95 | 49.95 | 13.50 | 57.00 |

**MRS RABBIT™**
**First Version (Umbrella Out)**

Modeller: Arthur Gredington
Height: 4 1/4", 10.8 cm
Colour: Pink and yellow striped dress, red collar and cap, yellow straw coloured basket
Issued: 1951 - c.1970

| *Back Stamp* | *Beswick Model* | *Doulton Number* | *U.S. $* | *Price Can. $* | *U.K.£* | *Aust. $* |
|---|---|---|---|---|---|---|
| BP-2 | 1200/1 | P1200/1 | 400.00 | 500.00 | 250.00 | 550.00 |
| BP-3 | | | 250.00 | 350.00 | 175.00 | 400.00 |

**MRS RABBIT™**
**Second Version (Umbrella Moulded to Dress)**

Modeller: Arthur Gredington
Height: 4 1/4", 10.8 cm
Colour: Rose-pink and yellow striped dress, red collar and cap, light straw coloured basket
Issued: c.1970 to the present

| *Back Stamp* | *Beswick Model* | *Doulton Number* | *U.S. $* | *Price Can. $* | *U.K. £* | *Aust. $* |
|---|---|---|---|---|---|---|
| BP-3 | 1200/2 | P1200/2 | 65.00 | 90.00 | 50.00 | 110.00 |
| BP-4 | | | 75.00 | 100.00 | 50.00 | 125.00 |
| BP-6 | | | 29.95 | 49.95 | 13.50 | 60.00 |

**MRS RABBIT™**
**Third Version (Large Size)**

Modeller: Martyn Alcock
Height: 6 1/4", 15.9 cm
Colour: White, pink, yellow and green
Issued: 1994

| *Back Stamp* | *Beswick Model* | *Doulton Number* | *U.S. $* | *Price Can. $* | *U.K. £* | *Aust. $* |
|---|---|---|---|---|---|---|
| BP-6 | 1200/3 | P1200/3 | 65.00 | 88.00 | 25.95 | 98.00 |

## MRS. RABBIT AND BUNNIES™

Modeller: David Lyttleton
Height: 3 3/4", 9.5 cm
Colour: Blue dress with white apron; dark blue chair
Issued: 1976 to the present

BEATRIX POTTER'S
Mrs. Rabbit and Bunnies
F Warne & Co Ltd
© Copyright 1976
BESWICK ENGLAND

| *Back Stamp* | *Beswick Model* | *Doulton Number* | *U.S. $* | *Price Can. $* | *U.K. £* | *Aust. $* |
|---|---|---|---|---|---|---|
| BP-3 | 2543 | P2543 | 85.00 | 125.00 | 45.00 | 130.00 |
| BP-4 | | | 95.00 | 140.00 | 50.00 | 150.00 |
| BP-5 | | | 100.00 | 150.00 | 50.00 | 160.00 |
| BP-6 | | | 29.95 | 49.95 | 13.50 | 60.00 |

## MRS. RABBIT COOKING™

Modeller: Martyn Alcock
Height: 4", 10.1 cm
Colour: Blue dress, white apron
Issued: 1992 to the present

ROYAL ALBERT ®
ENGLAND
Mrs Rabbit cooking
Beatrix Potter
© F WARNE & CO 1991
© 1992 ROYAL ALBERT LTD

| *Back Stamp* | *Beswick Model* | *Doulton Number* | *U.S. $* | *Price Can. $* | *U.K. £* | *Aust. $* |
|---|---|---|---|---|---|---|
| BP-6 | 3278 | P3278 | 29.95 | 49.95 | 13.50 | 62.00 |

## MRS TIGGY-WINKLE™
### First Version (Diagonal Stripes)

Modeller: Arthur Gredington
Height: 3 1/4", 8.3 cm
Colour: Red-brown and white dress, green and blue striped skirt, white apron
Issued: 1948 - c1970

BEATRIX POTTER'S
Mrs Tiggy-Winkle
Copyright
BESWICK ENGLAND

| *Back Stamp* | *Beswick Model* | *Doulton Number* | *U.S. $* | *Price Can.$* | *U.K. £* | *Aust. $* |
|---|---|---|---|---|---|---|
| BP-1 | 1107/1 | P1107/1 | 300.00 | 400.00 | 125.00 | 450.00 |
| BP-2 | | | 275.00 | 350.00 | 100.00 | 400.00 |
| BP-3 | | | 150.00 | 200.00 | 75.00 | 175.00 |

**MRS TIGGY-WINKLE™**
**Second Version (Square Stripes)**

Modeller: Arthur Gredington
Height: 3 1/4", 8.3 cm
Colour: Red-brown and white dress, green and blue striped skirt, white apron
Issued: c.1970 to the present

BEATRIX POTTER'S
"Mrs Tiggy Winkle"
F. Warne & Co. Ltd.
© Copyright 1948
BESWICK ENGLAND

| *Back Stamp* | *Beswick Model* | *Doulton No.* | *U.S. $* | *Price Can. $* | *U.K. £* | *Aust. $* |
|---|---|---|---|---|---|---|
| BP-3 | 1107/2 | P1107/2 | 85.00 | 125.00 | 45.00 | 135.00 |
| BP-4 | | | 95.00 | 135.00 | 45.00 | 150.00 |
| BP-5 | | | 100.00 | 150.00 | 50.00 | 160.00 |
| BP-6 | | | 29.95 | 49.95 | 13.50 | 60.00 |

**MRS. TIGGY-WINKLE CHARACTER JUG™**

Modeller: Ted Chawner
Height: 3", 7.6 cm
Colour: White dress with blue stripes
Issued: 1988 - 1992

| *Back Stamp* | *Beswick Model* | *Doulton Number* | *U.S. $* | *Price Can. $* | *U.K. £* | *Aust.* |
|---|---|---|---|---|---|---|
| BP-4 | 3102 | P3102 | 150.00 | 200.00 | 65.00 | 200.00 |
| BP-6 | | | 115.00 | 150.00 | 65.00 | 150.00 |

**MRS. TIGGY WINKLE TAKES TEA™**

Modeller: David Lyttleton
Height: 3 1/4", 8.3 cm
Colour: Pink and white dress, white and brown mob cap
Issued: 1985 to the present

ROYAL ALBERT ®
ENGLAND
Mrs. Tiggy Winkle
Takes Tea
Beatrix Potter
© F WARNE & CO 1985
C. 1989 ROYAL ALBERT LTD

| *Back Stamp* | *Beswick Model* | *Doulton Number* | *U.S. $* | *Price Can. $* | *U.K. £* | *Aust. $* |
|---|---|---|---|---|---|---|
| BP-3 | 2877 | P2877 | 85.00 | 150.00 | 95.00 | 150.00 |
| BP-4 | | | 95.00 | 175.00 | 125.00 | 175.00 |
| BP-6 | | | 29.95 | 49.95 | 13.50 | 57.00 |

## MRS TITTLEMOUSE™

Modeller: Arthur Gredington
Height: 3 1/2", 8.9 cm
Colour: White and red striped blouse; blue and white striped skirt
Issued: 1948 - 1993

| *Back Stamp* | *Beswick Model* | *Doulton Number* | *U.S. $* | *Price Can. $* | *U.K. £* | *Aust. $* |
|---|---|---|---|---|---|---|
| BP-1 | 1103 | P1103 | 300.00 | 450.00 | 110.00 | 450.00 |
| BP-2 | | | 250.00 | 350.00 | 95.00 | 350.00 |
| BP-3 | | | 65.00 | 100.00 | 60.00 | 110.00 |
| BP-4 | | | 75.00 | 110.00 | 60.00 | 125.00 |
| BP-6 | | | 35.00 | 50.00 | 25.00 | 60.00 |

## MRS. TITTLEMOUSE PLAQUE™

Modeller: Harry Sales
Height: 7 1/2" x 7 1/2", 19.1 cm x 19.1 cm
Colour: Unknown
Issued: 1982 - 1984

| *Back Stamp* | *Beswick Model* | *Doulton Number* | *U.S. $* | *Price Can. $* | *U.K. £* | *Aust. $* |
|---|---|---|---|---|---|---|
| BP-3 | 2685 | P2685 | 150.00 | 200.00 | 95.00 | 130.00 |

## NO MORE TWIST™

Modeller: Martyn Alcock
Height: 3 2/3", 9.2 cm
Colour: Brown and white mouse
Issued: 1992 to the present

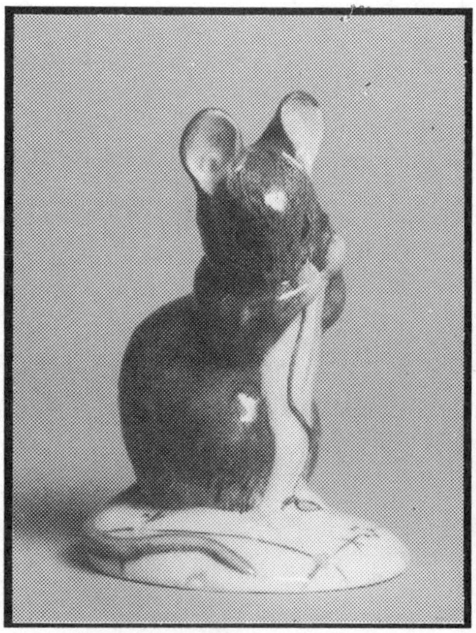

| *Back Stamp* | *Beswick Model* | *Doulton Number* | *U.S. $* | *Price Can. $* | *U.K. £* | *Aust. $* |
|---|---|---|---|---|---|---|
| BP-6 | 3325 | P3325 | 29.95 | 49.95 | 13.50 | 62.00 |

## OLD MR. BOUNCER™

Modeller: David Lyttleton
Height: 3", 7.6 cm
Colour: Brown jacket and trousers, blue scarf
Issued: 1986 to the present

BEATRIX POTTER
"Old Mr. Bouncer"
© Frederick Warne & Co. 1986
Licensed by Copyrights
BESWICK ENGLAND

| *Back Stamp* | *Beswick Model* | *Doulton Number* | *U.S. $* | *Price Can. $* | *U.K.£* | *Aust. $* |
|---|---|---|---|---|---|---|
| BP-3 | 2956 | P2956 | 65.00 | 90.00 | 45.00 | 100.00 |
| BP-4 | | | 75.00 | 110.00 | 50.00 | 125.00 |
| BP-6 | | | 29.95 | 49.95 | 13.50 | 64.00 |

## OLD MR BROWN™

Modeller: Albert Hallam
Height: 3 1/4", 8.3 cm
Colour: Brown owl and red squirrel
Issued: 1963 to the present

BEATRIX POTTER'S
"Old Mr Brown"
F. Warne & Co.Ltd.
© Copyright 1963
BESWICK ENGLAND

| *Back Stamp* | *Beswick Model* | *Doulton Number* | *U.S. $* | *Price Can. $* | *U.K. £* | *Aust. $* |
|---|---|---|---|---|---|---|
| BP-2 | 1796 | P1796 | 200.00 | 275.00 | 95.00 | 275.00 |
| BP-3 | | | 75.00 | 110.00 | 45.00 | 110.00 |
| BP-4 | | | 85.00 | 125.00 | 50.00 | 125.00 |
| BP-6 | | | 29.95 | 49.95 | 13.50 | 60.00 |

## OLD MR. BROWN CHARACTER JUG™

Modeller: Graham Tongue
Height: 3", 7.6 cm
Colour: Brown and cream
Issued: 1987 - 1992

John Beswick
ENGLAND
BEATRIX POTTER
"Old Mr. Brown"
© 1987 Frederick Warne & Co.
Licensed by Copyrights

| *Back Stamp* | *Beswick Model* | *Doulton Number* | *U.S. $* | *Price Can. $* | *U.K.* | *Aust. $* |
|---|---|---|---|---|---|---|
| BP-4 | 2959 | P2959 | 150.00 | 200.00 | 65.00 | 200.00 |
| BP-6 | | | 115.00 | 150.00 | 65.00 | 150.00 |

## OLD MR. PRICKLEPIN™

Modeller: David Lyttleton
Height: 2 1/2", 6.4 cm
Colour: Brown hedgehog
Issued: 1983 - 1989

BEATRIX POTTER'S
Old Mr Pricklepin
© Frederick Warne P.L.C. 1983
BESWICK ENGLAND

| *Back Stamp* | *Beswick Model* | *Doulton Number* | *U.S. $* | *Price Can. $* | *U.K. £* | *Aust. $* |
|---|---|---|---|---|---|---|
| BP-3 | 2767 | P2767 | 125.00 | 170.00 | 65.00 | 200.00 |
| BP-4 | | | 150.00 | 200.00 | 75.00 | 225.00 |
| BP-6 | | | 100.00 | 130.00 | 30.00 | 135.00 |

## PETER AND THE RED POCKET HANDKERCHIEF™

Modeller: Martyn Alcock
Height: 4 3/4", 12.3 cm
Colour: Brown blanket, light blue coat
Issued: 1991 to the present

ROYAL ALBERT ®
ENGLAND
Peter and the
Red Pocket Handkerchief
Beatrix Potter
© F. WARNE & CO. 1990
© 1990 ROYAL ALBERT LTD

| *Back Stamp* | *Beswick Model* | *Doulton Number* | *U.S. $* | *Price Can. $* | *U.K. £* | *Aust. $* |
|---|---|---|---|---|---|---|
| BP-6 | 3242 | P3242 | 45.00 | 59.95 | 15.95 | 68.00 |

## PETER RABBIT™

**First Version (Deep Light Blue Jacket)**

Modeller: Arthur Gredington
Height: 4 1/2", 11.4 cm
Colour: Brown and white rabbit wearing dark blue jacket
Issued: 1948 - c.1980

BEATRIX POTTER'S
Peter Rabbit
BESWICK
ENGLAND

| *Back Stamp* | *Beswick Model* | *Doulton Number* | *U.S. $* | *Price Can. $* | *U.K. £* | *Aust. $* |
|---|---|---|---|---|---|---|
| BP-1 | 1091/1 | P1091/1 | 275.00 | 400.00 | 145.00 | 450.00 |
| BP-2 | | | 250.00 | 325.00 | 125.00 | 350.00 |
| BP-3 | | | 150.00 | 200.00 | 75.00 | 225.00 |

## PETER RABBIT™
**Second Version (Pale Light Blue Jacket)**

Modeller: Arthur Gredington
Height: 4 1/2", 11.4 cm
Colour: Brown and white rabbit wearing light blue jacket
Issued: c. 1980 to the present

BEATRIX POTTER'S
"Peter Rabbit"
F. Warne & Co.Ltd.
© Copyright 1948
BESWICK ENGLAND

| *Back Stamp* | *Beswick Model* | *Doulton Number* | *U.S. $* | *Price Can. $* | *U.K. £* | *Aust. $* |
|---|---|---|---|---|---|---|
| BP-3 | 1098/2 | P1098/2 | 65.00 | 90.00 | 45.00 | 100.00 |
| BP-4 | | | 75.00 | 110.00 | 45.00 | 125.00 |
| BP-5 | | | 100.00 | 140.00 | 50.00 | 150.00 |
| BP-6 | | | 29.95 | 49.95 | 13.50 | 57.00 |

BEATRIX POTTER'S
Peter Rabbit™
© F. WARNE & CO.1992
© 1992 ROYAL DOULTON
PETER RABBIT 1893 100 1993 F. WARNE & Co.
BESWICK ENGLAND

## PETER RABBIT™
**Third Version (Large size)**

Modeller: Martyn Alcock
Height: 6 3/4", 17.1 cm
Size: Large
Colour: Brown rabbit wearing a blue coat
Issued: 1993 to the present

| *Back Stamp* | *Beswick Model* | *Doulton Number* | *U.S. $* | *Price Can. $* | *U.K. £* | *Aust. $* |
|---|---|---|---|---|---|---|
| BP-6 | | | 65.00 | 100.00 | 30.00 | 98.00 |
| BP-7 1993 100th Anniversary | | | 95.00 | 125.00 | 50.00 | 140.00 |

## PETER RABBIT CHARACTER JUG™

Modeller: Graham Tongue
Height: 3", 7.6 cm
Colour: Brown, blue and white
Issued: 1987 - 1992

John Beswick
ENGLAND
BEATRIX POTTER
"Peter Rabbit"
© 1987 Frederick Warne & Co.
Licensed by Copyrights

| *Back Stamp* | *Beswick Model* | *Doulton Number* | *U.S. $* | *Price Can. $* | *U.K. £* | *Aust. $* |
|---|---|---|---|---|---|---|
| BP-4 | | | 150.00 | 210.00 | 75.00 | 225.00 |
| BP-6 | | | 115.00 | 165.00 | 65.00 | 175.00 |

**PETER RABBIT IN THE GOOSEBERRY NET™**

Modeller: David Lyttleton
Height: 2", 4.6 cm
Colour: Brown and white rabbit wearing blue jacket, green netting
Issued: 1989 to the present

ROYAL ALBERT ®
ENGLAND
Peter in the Gooseberry Net
Beatrix Potter
© F. WARNE & CO. 1989
© 1989 ROYAL ALBERT LTD

| *Back Stamp* | *Beswick Model* | *Doulton Number* | *U.S. $* | *Price Can. $* | *U.K. £* | *Aust. $* |
|---|---|---|---|---|---|---|
| BP-6 | 3157 | P3157 | 50.00 | 69.95 | 16.95 | 68.00 |

**PETER RABBIT PLAQUE™**
**First Version**

Modeller: Graham Tongue
Height: 6", 15.2 cm
Colour: Blue jacket, orange carrot, brown earth, green foliage and blue sky
Issued: 1967 - 1969

| *Back Stamp* | *Beswick Model* | *Doulton Number* | *U.S. $* | *Price Can. $* | *U.K. £* | *Aust. $* |
|---|---|---|---|---|---|---|
| BP-2 | 2083 | P2083 | | Extremely Rare | | |

**PETER RABBIT PLAQUE™**
**Second Version**

Modeller: Harry Sales and David Lyttleton
Height: 7 1/2" x 7 1/2", 19.1 cm x 19.1 cm
Colour: Unknown
Issued: 1979 - 1983

*Photograph Not Available At Press Time*

| *Back Stamp* | *Beswick Model* | *Doulton Number* | *U.S. $* | *Price Can. $* | *U.K. £* | *Aust. $* |
|---|---|---|---|---|---|---|
| BP-3 | 2650 | P2650 | 145.00 | 150.00 | 75.00 | 160.00 |

## PICKLES™

Modeller: Albert Hallam
Height: 4 1/2", 11.4 cm
Colour: Black face dog with brown jacket and white apron, pink book
Issued: 1971 - 1982

| *Back Stamp* | *Beswick Model* | *Doulton Number* | *U.S. $* | *Price Can. $* | *U.K. £* | *Aust. $* |
|---|---|---|---|---|---|---|
| BP-2 | 2334 | P2334 | 750.00 | 1,000.00 | 280.00 | 1,000.00 |
| BP-3 | | | 425.00 | 600.00 | 250.00 | 650.00 |

## PIGLING BLAND™
### First Version (Deep Maroon Jacket)

Modeller: Graham Orwell
Height: 4 1/4", 10.8 cm
Colour: Purple jacket, blue waistcoat, yellow trousers
Issued: 1955 - c.1970

| *Back Stamp* | *Beswick Model* | *Doulton Number* | *U.S. $* | *Price Can. $* | *U.K. £* | *Aust. $* |
|---|---|---|---|---|---|---|
| BP-2 | 1365/1 | P1365/1 | 600.00 | 800.00 | 275.00 | 850.00 |

## PIGLING BLAND™
### Second Version (Lilac Jacket)

Modeller: Graham Orwell
Height: 4 1/4", 10.8 cm
Colour: Lilac jacket, blue waistcoat, yellow trousers
Issued: c.1970 to the present

| *Back Stamp* | *Beswick Model* | *Doulton Number* | *U.S. $* | *Price Can. $* | *U.K. £* | *Aust. $* |
|---|---|---|---|---|---|---|
| BP-2 | 1365/2 | 1365/2 | 295.00 | 350.00 | 175.00 | 350.00 |
| BP-3 | | | 65.00 | 90.00 | 50.00 | 100.00 |
| BP-4 | | | 75.00 | 110.00 | 60.00 | 125.00 |
| BP-6 | | | 29.95 | 49.95 | 13.50 | 80.00 |

## PIGLING EATS HIS PORRIDGE™

Modeller: Martyn Alcock
Height: 4", 10.1 cm
Colour: Brown coat, blue waistcoat and yellow trousers
Issued: 1991 - 1994

ROYAL ALBERT ®
ENGLAND
Pigling Eats His Porridge
Beatrix Potter
© F WARNE & CO 1991
© 1991 ROYAL ALBERT LTD

| Back Stamp | Beswick Model | Doulton Number | U.S. $ | Price Can. $ | U.K. £ | Aust. $ |
|---|---|---|---|---|---|---|
| BP-6 | 3252 | P3252 | 50.00 | 69.95 | 16.95 | 83.00 |

## PIG-WIG™

Modeller: Albert Hallam
Height: 4", 10.1 cm
Colour: Blue dress with white collar, black pig
Issued: 1972 - 1982

BEATRIX POTTER'S
"PIGWIG"
F. WARNE & CO.LTD.
© Copyright 1972
BESWICK
ENGLAND

| Back Stamp | Beswick Model | Doulton Number | U.S. $ | Price Can. $ | U.K. £ | Aust. $ |
|---|---|---|---|---|---|---|
| BP-2 | 2381 | P2382 | | Extremely Rare | | |
| BP-3 | | | 600.00 | 850.00 | 400.00 | 900.00 |

## POORLY PETER RABBIT™

Modeller: David Lyttleton
Height: 3 3/4", 9.5 cm
Colour: Brown-red and white blanket
Issued: 1976 to the present

BEATRIX POTTER
"Poorly Peter Rabbit"
© Frederick Warne & Co. 1976
Licensed by Copyrights
BESWICK ENGLAND

| Back Stamp | Beswick Model | Doulton Number | U.S. $ | Price Can. $ | U.K. £ | Aust. $ |
|---|---|---|---|---|---|---|
| BP-3 | 2560 | P2560 | 65.00 | 90.00 | 45.00 | 100.00 |
| BP-4 | | | 75.00 | 110.00 | 50.00 | 125.00 |
| BP-6 | | | 45.00 | 50.00 | 20.00 | 57.00 |

## REBECCAH PUDDLE-DUCK™

Modeller: David Lyttleton
Height: 3 1/4", 8.3 cm
Colour: White goose, pale blue coat and hat
Issued: 1981 to the present

| Back Stamp | Beswick Model | Doulton Number | U.S. $ | Price Can. $ | U.K. £ | Aust. |
|---|---|---|---|---|---|---|
| BP-3 | 2647 | P2647 | 65.00 | 90.00 | 45.00 | 100.00 |
| BP-4 | | | 75.00 | 110.00 | 45.00 | 125.00 |
| BP-6 | | | 29.95 | 49.95 | 13.50 | 70.00 |

## RIBBY™

Modeller: Arthur Gredington
Height: 3 1/4", 8.3 cm
Colour: White dress with blue rings, white apron, pink and white striped shawl
Issued: 1951 to the present

| Back Stamp | Beswick Model | Doulton Number | U.S. $ | Price Can. $ | U.K. £ | Aust. $ |
|---|---|---|---|---|---|---|
| BP-2 | 1199 | P1199 | 225.00 | 300.00 | 110.00 | 325.00 |
| BP-3 | | | 65.00 | 90.00 | 45.00 | 100.00 |
| BP-4 | | | 75.00 | 110.00 | 55.00 | 125.00 |
| BP-6 | | | 29.95 | 49.95 | 13.50 | 57.00 |

## RIBBY AND THE PATTY PAN™

Modeller: Martyn Alcock
Height: 3 1/2", 8.9 cm
Colour: Blue dress, white apron
Issued: 1992 to the present

| Back Stamp | Beswick Model | Doulton Number | U.S. $ | Price Can. $ | U.K. £ | Aust. $ |
|---|---|---|---|---|---|---|
| BP-6 | 3280 | P3280 | 29.95 | 49.95 | 13.50 | 57.00 |

**SALLY HENNY PENNY™**
**First Version (Mouth Open)**

Modeller: Albert Hallam
Height: 4", 10.1 cm
Colour: Brown and gold chicken, black hat and cloak, two yellow chicks
Issued: 1974 - 1980's

BEATRIX POTTER'S
Sally Henny Penny
F. Warne & Co.Ltd.
© Copyright 1974
BESWICK ENGLAND

*Photograph Not Available At Press Time*

| *Back Stamp* | *Beswick Model* | *Doulton Number* | *Price U.S. $* | *Can. $* | *U.K. £* | *Aust. $* |
|---|---|---|---|---|---|---|
| BP-3 | 2452 | P2452 | 150.00 | 225.00 | 100.00 | 250.00 |

**SALLY HENNY PENNY™**
**Second Version (Mouth Closed)**

Modeller: Albert Hallam
Height: 4", 10.1 cm
Colour: Brown and gold chicken, black hat and cloak, two yellow chicks
Issued: 1980's to 1993

| *Back Stamp* | *Beswick Model* | *Doulton Number* | *Price U.S. $* | *Can. $* | *U.K. £* | *Aust. $* |
|---|---|---|---|---|---|---|
| BP-3 | 2452 | P2452 | 65.00 | 90.00 | 45.00 | 100.00 |
| BP-4 | | | 75.00 | 110.00 | 50.00 | 125.00 |
| BP-6 | | | 45.00 | 60.00 | 30.00 | 84.00 |

**SAMUEL WHISKERS™**

Modeller: Arthur Gredington
Height: 3 1/4", 8.3 cm
Colour: Light green coat, yellow waistcoat and trousers
Issued: 1948 to the present

BEATRIX POTTERS

| *Back Stamp* | *Beswick Model* | *Doulton Number* | *Price U.S. $* | *Can. $* | *U.K. £* | *Aust. $* |
|---|---|---|---|---|---|---|
| BP-1 | 1106 | P1106 | 300.00 | 425.00 | 130.00 | 450.00 |
| BP-2 | | | 275.00 | 350.00 | 115.00 | 375.00 |
| BP-3 | | | 65.00 | 90.00 | 45.00 | 100.00 |
| BP-4 | | | 75.00 | 110.00 | 45.00 | 125.00 |
| BP-6 | | | 29.95 | 49.95 | 13.50 | 57.00 |

## SIMPKIN™

Modeller: Alan Maslankowski
Height: 4", 10.1 cm
Colour: Green coat
Issued: 1975 - 1983

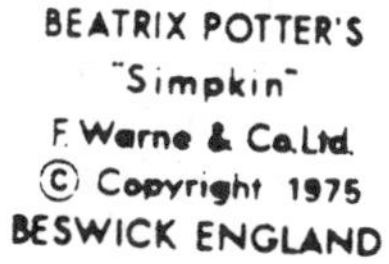


| Back Stamp | Beswick Model | Doulton Number | U.S. $ | Price Can. $ | U.K. £ | Aust. $ |
|---|---|---|---|---|---|---|
| BP-3 | 2508 | P2508 | 900.00 | 1,200.00 | 500.00 | 1,250.00 |

## SIR ISAAC NEWTON™

Modeller: Graham Tongue
Height: 3 3/4", 9.5 cm
Colour: Pale green jacket yellow waistcoat with tan markings
Issued: 1973 - 1984

| Back Stamp | Beswick Model | Doulton Number | U.S. $ | Price Can. $ | U.K. £ | Aust. $ |
|---|---|---|---|---|---|---|
| BP-3 | 2425 | P2425 | 500.00 | 600.00 | 300.00 | 650.00 |

## SQUIRREL NUTKIN™
**First Version (Red Brown Squirrel)**

Modeller: Arthur Gredington
Height: 3 3/4", 9.5 cm
Colour: Red-brown squirrel holding green-brown nut
Issued: 1948 - c.1980

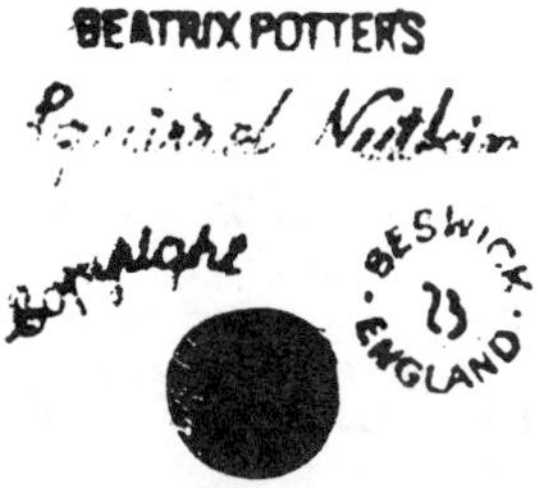


| Back Stamp | Beswick Model | Doulton Number | U.S. $ | Price Can. $ | U.K. £ | Aust. $ |
|---|---|---|---|---|---|---|
| BP-1 | 1102 | P1102/1 | 275.00 | 350.00 | 150.00 | 375.00 |
| BP-2 | | | 250.00 | 300.00 | 125.00 | 325.00 |
| BP-3 | | | 150.00 | 200.00 | 95.00 | 225.00 |

## SQUIRREL NUTKIN™
**Second Version (Golden Brown Squirrel)**

Modeller: Arthur Gredington
Height: 3 3/4", 9.5 cm
Colour: Golden-brown squirrel holding green nut
Issued: c.1980 to the present

BEATRIX POTTER'S
"Squirrel Nutkin"
F. Warne & Co.Ltd.
© Copyright 1948
BESWICK
ENGLAND

| Back Stamp | Beswick Model | Doulton Number | Price U.S. $ | Can. $ | U.K. £ | Aust. $ |
|---|---|---|---|---|---|---|
| BP-3 | 1102 | P1102/2 | 65.00 | 90.00 | 40.00 | 100.00 |
| BP-4 | | | 75.00 | 110.00 | 45.00 | 125.00 |
| BP-6 | | | 29.95 | 49.95 | 13.50 | 64.00 |

## SUSAN™

Modeller: David Lyttleton
Height: 4", 10.1 cm
Colour: Blue dress, green, pink and black shawl and hat
Issued: 1983 - 1989

BEATRIX POTTER'S
"Susan"
© Frederick Warne P.L.C. 1983
BESWICK ENGLAND

| Back Stamp | Beswick Model | Doulton Number | Price U.S. $ | Can. $ | U.K. £ | Aust. $ |
|---|---|---|---|---|---|---|
| BP-3 | 2716 | P2716 | 200.00 | 275.00 | 95.00 | 300.00 |
| BP-4 | | | 75.00 | 110.00 | 85.00 | 125.00 |
| BP-6 | | | 150.00 | 200.00 | 75.00 | 200.00 |

## TABITHA TWITCHIT™
**First Version (Blue Striped Top)**

Modeller: Arthur Gredington
Height: 3 1/2", 8.9 cm
Colour: Blue and white striped dress, white apron
Issued: 1961 - c.1970

BEATRIX POTTER'S
Tabitha Twitchit
F. WARNE & CO. LTD.
COPYRIGHT
BESWICK
ENGLAND

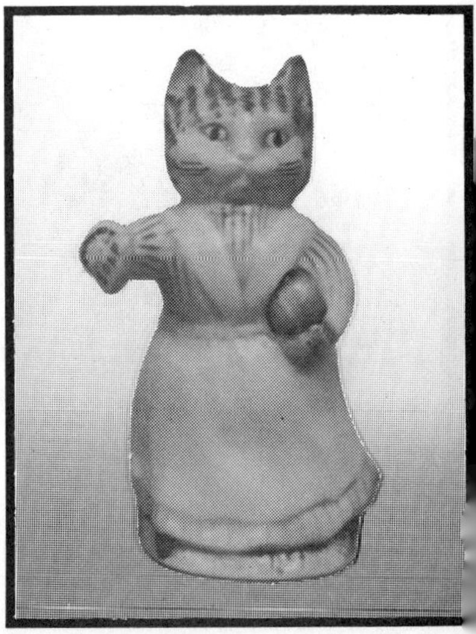

| Back Stamp | Beswick Model | Doulton Number | Price U.S. $ | Can. $ | U.K. £ | Aust. $ |
|---|---|---|---|---|---|---|
| BP-2 | 1676/1 | P1676/1 | 275.00 | 350.00 | 125.00 | 375.00 |
| BP-3 | | | 275.00 | 350.00 | 125.00 | 375.00 |

**TABITHA TWITCHIT™**
**Second Version (White Top)**

Modeller: Arthur Gredington
Height: 3 1/2", 8.9 cm
Colour: Blue and white striped dress, white apron
Issued: c.1970 to the present

BEATRIX POTTER'S
"Tabitha Twitchett"
F. Warne & Co.Ltd.
© Copyright 1961
BESWICK ENGLAND

Note: BP-3 and forward has Twitchett spelt with two "T"s

| *Back Stamp* | *Beswick Model* | *Doulton Number* | *U.S. $* | *Price Can. $* | *U.K. £* | *Aust. $* |
|---|---|---|---|---|---|---|
| BP-2 | 1676/2 | P1676/2 | 250.00 | 325.00 | 140.00 | 350.00 |
| BP-3 | | | 65.00 | 90.00 | 45.00 | 100.00 |
| BP-4 | | | 75.00 | 110.00 | 50.00 | 125.00 |
| BP-6 | | | 29.95 | 49.95 | 13.50 | 64.00 |

**TABITHA TWITCHIT AND MISS MOPPET™**

Modeller: David Lyttleton
Height: 3 1/2", 8.9 cm
Colour: Lilac dress, white apron, yellow sponge and puffee
Issued: 1976 - 1993

BEATRIX POTTER'S
Tabitha Twitchit and Miss Moppet
F. Warne & Co.Ltd.
© Copyright 1976
BESWICK ENGLAND

| *Back Stamp* | *Beswick* | *Doulton Number* | *U.S. $* | *Price Can. $* | *U.K. £* | *Aust. $* |
|---|---|---|---|---|---|---|
| BP-3 | 2544 | P2544 | 200.00 | 275.00 | 155.00 | 300.00 |
| BP-4 | | | 250.00 | 350.00 | 175.00 | 375.00 |
| BP-6 | | | 75.00 | 110.00 | 50.00 | 125.00 |

**TAILOR OF GLOUCESTER™**

Modeller: Arthur Gredington
Height: 3 1/2", 8.9 cm
Colour: Brown mouse, yellow bobbin of red thread
Issued: 1949 to the present

BEATRIX POTTERS
Tailor of Gloucester
BESWICK ENGLAND
F. WARNE & CO. LTD.
COPYRIGHT

| *Back Stamp* | *Beswick Model* | *Doulton Number* | *U.S. $* | *Price Can. $* | *U.K. £* | *Aust. $* |
|---|---|---|---|---|---|---|
| BP-2 | 1108 | P1108 | 250.00 | 350.00 | 100.00 | 375.00 |
| BP-3 | | | 65.00 | 90.00 | 45.00 | 100.00 |
| BP-4 | | | 75.00 | 110.00 | 45.00 | 125.00 |
| BP-6 | | | 29.95 | 49.95 | 13.50 | 57.00 |

## THE OLD WOMAN WHO LIVED IN A SHOE™

Modeller: Colin Melbourne
Height: 2 3/4" x 3 3/4", 7 cm x 9.5 cm
Colour: Blue shoe
Issued: 1959 to the present

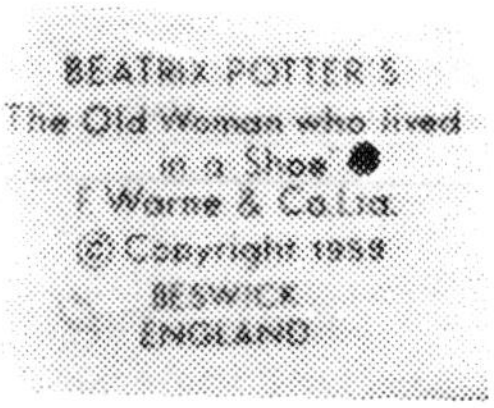


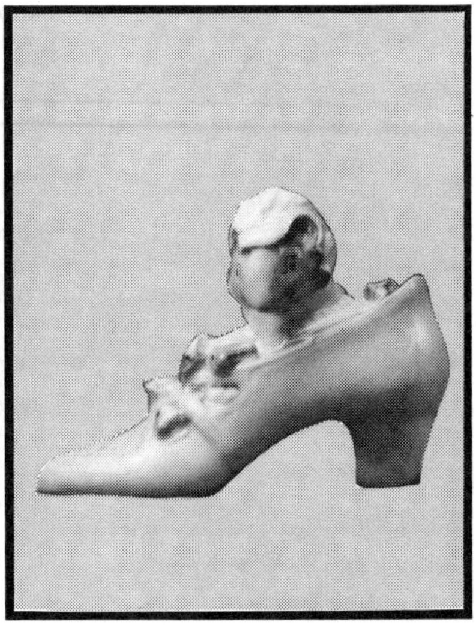

| *Back Stamp* | *Beswick Model* | *Doulton Number* | *U.S. $* | *Price Can. $* | *U.K. £* | *Aust. $* |
|---|---|---|---|---|---|---|
| BP-2 | 1545 | P1545 | 225.00 | 300.00 | 95.00 | 325.00 |
| BP-3 | | | 65.00 | 90.00 | 45.00 | 90.00 |
| BP-4 | | | 75.00 | 110.00 | 50.00 | 110.00 |
| BP-6 | | | 29.95 | 49.95 | 13.50 | 84.00 |

## THE OLD WOMAN WHO LIVED IN A SHOE KNITTING™

Modeller: David Lyttleton
Height: 3", 7.5 cm
Colour: Purple dress, white apron, pale blue shawl and mob cap, yellow chair
Issued: 1983 to the present

BEATRIX POTTER
"The Old Woman who lived
in a Shoe.
"Knitting"
© Frederick Warne & Co. 1983
Licensed by Copyrights
BESWICK ENGLAND

| *Back Stamp* | *Beswick Model* | *Doulton Number* | *U.S. $* | *Price Can. $* | *U.K.£* | *Aust. $* |
|---|---|---|---|---|---|---|
| BP-3 | 2804 | P2804 | 250.00 | 350.00 | 160.00 | 375.00 |
| BP-4 | | | 275.00 | 375.00 | 160.00 | 400.00 |
| BP-6 | | | 29.95 | 49.95 | 13.50 | 64.00 |

## THOMASINA TITTLEMOUSE™

Modeller: David Lyttleton
Height: 3 1/4", 8.3 cm
Colour: Brown and pink Highlights
Issued: 1981 - 1990

BEATRIX POTTER'S
"Thomasina Tittlemouse
F. Warne & Co Ltd.
© Copyright 1981
BESWICK ENGLAND

BEATRIX POTTER
"Tomasina Tittlemouse"
© Frederick Warne & Co. 1981
Licensed by Copyrights
BESWICK ENGLAND

Correct Error
Backstamp Variations

| *Back Stamp* | *Beswick Model* | *Doulton Number* | *U.S. $* | *Price Can. $* | *U.K. £* | *Aust. $* |
|---|---|---|---|---|---|---|
| BP-3 Correct | 2668 | P2668 | 125.00 | 175.00 | 60.00 | 200.00 |
| BP-3 Error | | | 125.00 | 175.00 | 60.00 | 200.00 |
| BP-4 | | | 150.00 | 200.00 | 100.00 | 225.00 |
| BP-6 | | | 100.00 | 65.00 | 35.00 | 64.00 |

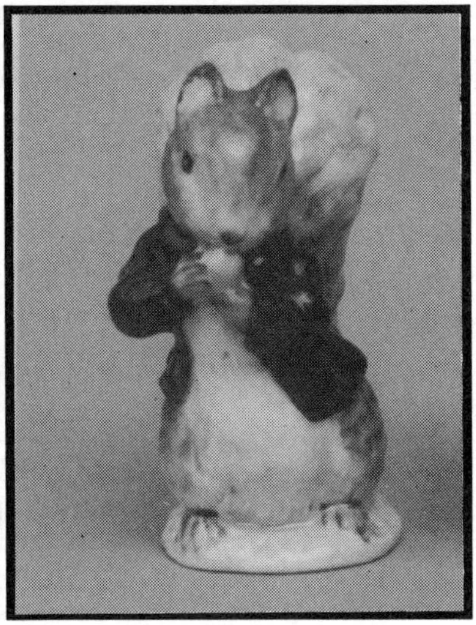

## TIMMY TIPTOES™
**First Version (Red Jacket)**

BEATRIX POTTER'S
Timmy Tiptoes
F. WARNE & CO. LTD.
COPYRIGHT
BESWICK
ENGLAND

| | |
|---|---|
| Modeller: | Arthur Gredington |
| Height: | 3 3/4", 9.5 cm |
| Colour: | Grey squirrel with brown shading , wearing red jacket |
| Issued: | 1948 - c.1980 |

| *Back Stamp* | *Beswick Model* | *Doulton Number* | *U.S. $* | *Price Can. $* | *U.K. £* | *Aust. $* |
|---|---|---|---|---|---|---|
| BP-1 | 1101 | P1101/1 | 250.00 | 350.00 | 125.00 | 375.00 |
| BP-2 | | | 225.00 | 300.00 | 115.00 | 325.00 |
| BP-3 | | | 150.00 | 200.00 | 85.00 | 225.00 |

## TIMMY TIPTOES™
**Second Version (Light Pink Jacket)**

| | |
|---|---|
| Modeller: | Arthur Gredington |
| Height: | 3 1/2", 8.9 cm |
| Colour: | Grey squirrel wearing pink jacket |
| Issued: | c.1980 to the present |

BEATRIX POTTER'S
"Timmy Tiptoes"
F. Warne & Co.Ltd.
(C) Copyright 1948
BESWICK ENGLAND

| *Back Stamp* | *Beswick Model* | *Doulton Number* | *U.S. $* | *Price Can. $* | *U.K. £* | *Aust. $* |
|---|---|---|---|---|---|---|
| BP-3 | 1101 | P1101/2 | 65.00 | 90.00 | 40.00 | 100.00 |
| BP-4 | | | 75.00 | 110.00 | 45.00 | 125.00 |
| BP-6 | | | 29.95 | 49.95 | 13.50 | 64.00 |

## TIMMY WILLIE FROM JOHNNY TOWN-MOUSE™

F. WARNE & CO. LTD.
COPYRIGHT
BEATRIX POTTER'S
"Timmy Willie" from Johnny Town-Mouse
BESWICK
ENGLAND

| | |
|---|---|
| Modeller: | Arthur Gredington |
| Height: | 2 1/2", 6.4 cm |
| Colour: | Brown and white mouse, green base |
| Issued: | 1949 - 1993 |

| *Back Stamp* | *Beswick Model* | *Doulton Number* | *U.S. $* | *Price Can. $* | *U.K. £* | *Aust. $* |
|---|---|---|---|---|---|---|
| BP-1 | 1109 | P1109 | 250.00 | 350.00 | 125.00 | 375.00 |
| BP-2 | | | 225.00 | 300.00 | 115.00 | 325.00 |
| BP-3 | | | 65.00 | 90.00 | 50.00 | 100.00 |
| BP-4 | | | 75.00 | 110.00 | 55.00 | 125.00 |
| BP-6 | | | 45.00 | 49.95 | 25.00 | 57.00 |

**TIMMY WILLIE SLEEPING™**

Modeller: Graham Tongue
Height: 1 1/4" x 3 3/4", 3.2 cm x 9.5 cm
Colour: Green, white and brown
Issued: 1986 to the present

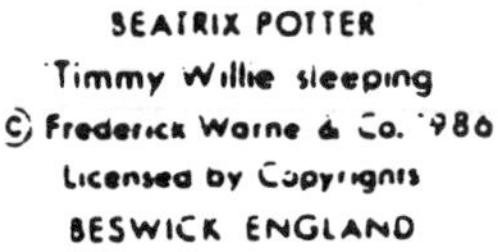


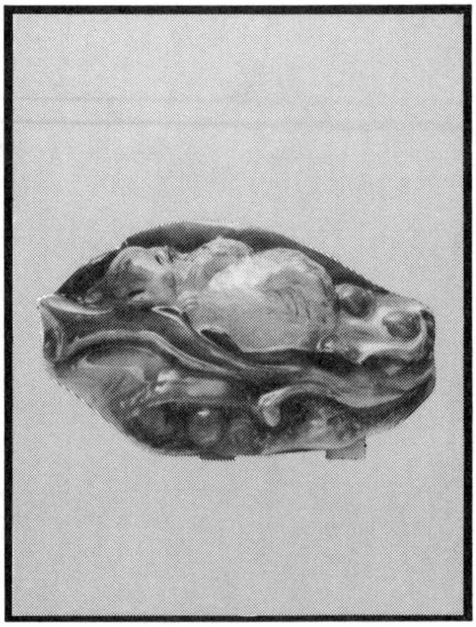

| *Back Stamp* | *Beswick Model* | *Doulton Number* | *U.S. $* | *Price Can. $* | *U.K. £* | *Aust. $* |
|---|---|---|---|---|---|---|
| BP-3 | 2996 | P2996 | 175.00 | 250.00 | 115.00 | 275.00 |
| BP-4 | | | 200.00 | 275.00 | 125.00 | 300.00 |
| BP-6 | | | 29.95 | 49.95 | 13.50 | 64.00 |

**TOM KITTTEN™**
**First Version (Deep Light Blue Outfit)**

Modeller: Arthur Gredington
Height: 3 1/2", 8.9 cm
Colour: Tabby kitten wearing light blue trousers and jacket; dark green base
Issued: 1948-c.1980

| *Back Stamp* | *Beswick Model* | *Doulton Number* | *U.S. $* | *Price Can. $* | *U.K. £* | *Aus.t $* |
|---|---|---|---|---|---|---|
| BP-1 | 1100 | P1100/1 | 275.00 | 400.00 | 125.00 | 425.00 |
| BP-2 | | | 225.00 | 300.00 | 115.00 | 325.00 |
| BP-3 | | | 65.00 | 90.00 | 45.00 | 120.00 |

**TOM KITTEN™**
**Second Version (Pale Light Blue Outfit)**

Modeller: Arthur Gredington
Height: 3 1/2", 8.9 cm
Colour: Tabby kitten wearing dark blue trousers and jacket; light green base
Issued: c.1980 to the present

| *Back Stamp* | *Beswick Model* | *Doulton Number* | *U.S. $* | *Price Can. $* | *U.K. £* | *Aust. $* |
|---|---|---|---|---|---|---|
| BP-3 | 1100 | P1100/2 | 65.00 | 90.00 | 45.00 | 100.00 |
| BP-4 | | | 75.00 | 110.00 | 55.00 | 125.00 |
| BP-6 | | | 29.95 | 49.95 | 13.50 | 57.00 |

**TOM KITTEN™**
**Third Version (Large size)**

Modeller: Martyn Alcock
Height: 5 1/4", 13.3 cm
Colour: Tabby kitten wearing light blue trousers and jacket; light green base
Issued: 1994

| *Back Stamp* | *Beswick Model* | *Doulton Number* | *U.S. $* | *Price Can. $* | *U.K. £* | *Aus.t $* |
|---|---|---|---|---|---|---|
| BP- | 1100 | P1100/3 | 65.00 | 88.00 | 25.95 | 98.00 |

**TOM KITTEN AND BUTTERFLY™**

Modeller: Ted Chawner
Height: 3 1/2", 8.9 cm
Colour: Blue outfit, yellow hat
Issued: 1987 - 1994

| *Back Stamp* | *Beswick Model* | *Doulton Number* | *U.S. $* | *Price Can. $* | *U.K. £* | *Aust. $* |
|---|---|---|---|---|---|---|
| BP-3 | 3030 | P3030 | 225.00 | 300.00 | 175.00 | 325.00 |
| BP-4 | | | 250.00 | 350.00 | 175.00 | 375.00 |
| BP-6 | | | 50.00 | 69.95 | 15.95 | 90.00 |

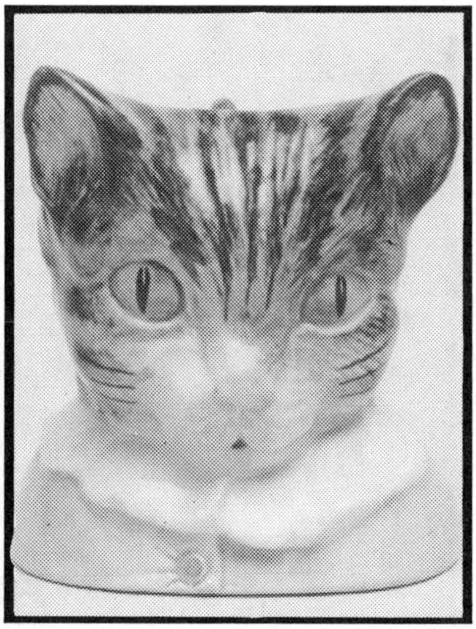

**TOM KITTEN CHARACTER JUG™**

Modeller: Ted Chawner
Height: 3", 7.6 cm
Colour: Brown, blue and white
Issued: 1989 - 1992

| *Back Stamp* | *Beswick Model* | *Doulton Number* | *U.S. $* | *Price Can. $* | *U.K. £* | *Aust. $* |
|---|---|---|---|---|---|---|
| BP-4 | | | 150.00 | 200.00 | 75.00 | 80.00 |
| BP-6 | | | 115.00 | 150.00 | 65.00 | 80.00 |

### TOM KITTEN PLAQUE™

Modeller: Graham Tongue
Height: 6", 15.2 cm
Colour: Unknown
Issued: 1967 - 1969

| Back Stamp | Beswick Model | Doulton Number | U.S. $ | Price Can. $ | U.K. | Aust. $ |
|---|---|---|---|---|---|---|
| BP-2 | 2085 | P2085 | | Extremely Rare | | |

*Photograph Not Available At Press Time*

### TOM THUMB™

Modeller: Warren Platt
Height: 3 1/4", 8.3 cm
Colour: Rose-pink and yellow chimney
Issued: 1987 to the present

BEATRIX POTTER
"Tom Thumb"
© F. Warne & Co. 1987
Licensed by Copyrights
BESWICK ENGLAND

| Back Stamp | Beswick Model | Doulton Number | U.S. $ | Price Can. $ | U.K. £ | Aust. $ |
|---|---|---|---|---|---|---|
| BP-3 | 2989 | P2989 | 165.00 | 225.00 | 100.00 | 250.00 |
| BP-4 | | | 165.00 | 225.00 | 100.00 | 250.00 |
| BP-6 | | | 29.95 | 49.95 | 13.50 | 64.00 |

### TOMMY BROCK
**First Version (Handle Out, Small Eye Patch)™**

Modeller: Graham Orwell
Height: 3 1/2", 8.9 cm
Colour: Blue jacket, pink waistcoat, yellow-green trousers
Issued: 1955 - c.1970

BEATRIX POTTER'S
"Tommy Brock
F. Warne & Co.Ltd.
© Copyright 1955
BESWICK ENGLAND

| Back Stamp | Beswick Model | Doulton Number | U.S. $ | Price Can. $ | U.K. £ | Aust. $ |
|---|---|---|---|---|---|---|
| BP-2 | 1348/1 | P1348/1 | 625.00 | 900.00 | 275.00 | 1,000.00 |
| BP-3 | | | 525.00 | 800.00 | 250.00 | 900.00 |

**TOMMY BROCK™**
**Second Version (Handle Out, Large Eye Patch)**

Modeller: Graham Orwell
Height: 3 1/2", 8.9 cm
Colour: Blue jacket, pink waistcoat, yellow trousers
Issued: c.1970 - c.1980

BEATRIX POTTER'S
"Tommy Brock"
F. Warne & Co.Ltd.
© Copyright 1955
BESWICK ENGLAND

| *Back Stamp* | *Beswick Model* | *Doulton Number* | *U.S. $* | *Price Can. $* | *U.K. £* | *Aust. $* |
|---|---|---|---|---|---|---|
| BP-2 | 1348/2 | P1348/2 | 625.00 | 900.00 | 275.00 | 1,000.00 |
| BP-3 | | | 525.00 | 800.00 | 250.00 | 900.00 |

**TOMMY BROCK™**
**Third Version (Handle in, Small Eye Patch)**

Modeller: Graham Orwell
Height: 3 1/2", 8.9 cm
Colour: Blue-grey jacket, pink waistcoat, yellow trousers
Issued: c.1980 to the present

BEATRIX POTTER'S
"Tommy Brock"
F. Warne & Co.Ltd.
© Copyright 1955
BESWICK ENGLAND

| *Back Stamp* | *Beswick Model* | *Doulton Number* | *U.S. $* | *Price Can. $* | *U.K. £* | *Aust. $* |
|---|---|---|---|---|---|---|
| BP-2 | 1348 | P1348/3 | 295.00 | 425.00 | 200.00 | 450.00 |
| BP-3 | | | 65.00 | 90.00 | 45.00 | 100.00 |

**TOMMY BROCK™**
**Fourth Version (Handle in, Large Eye Patch)**

Modeller: Graham Orwell
Height: 3 1/2", 8.9 cm
Colour: Blue-grey jacket, red waistcoat, yellow trousers
Issued: c.1980 to the present

BEATRIX POTTER'S
"Tommy Brock"
F. Warne & Co.Ltd.
© Copyright 1955
BESWICK ENGLAND

| *Back Stamp* | *Beswick Model* | *Doulton Number* | *U.S. $* | *Price Can. $* | *U.K. £* | *Aust. $* |
|---|---|---|---|---|---|---|
| BP-3 | 1348 | P1348/4 | 65.00 | 90.00 | 45.00 | 100.00 |
| BP-4 | | | 75.00 | 110.00 | 50.00 | 125.00 |
| BP-6 | | | 29.95 | 49.95 | 13.50 | 68.00 |

**TREE LAMP BASE™**

Modeller: James Hayward and Albert Hallam
Height: 7", 17.8 cm
Colour: Brown and green
Issued: 1958 - 1982

| *Back Stamp* | *Beswick Model* | *Doulton Number* | *U.S. $* | *Price Can. $* | *U.K. £* | *Aust. $* |
|---|---|---|---|---|---|---|
| BP-2 | 1531 | P1531 | 275.00 | 375.00 | 175.00 | 400.00 |
| BP-3 | | | 225.00 | 300.00 | 125.00 | 325.00 |

*BRAMBLY HEDGE*

**DBH1**
**POPPY EYEBRIGHT™**

Designer: Harry Sales
Modeller: David Lyttleton
Height: 3 1/4", 9.5 cm
Colour: Grey-white and pink dress, white apron trimmed with blue flowers
Issued: 1982 to the present

Royal Doulton
POPPY EYEBRIGHT

| *Back Stamp* | *U.S. $* | *Price Can. $* | *U.K. £* | *Aust. $* |
|---|---|---|---|---|
| BH-1 | 40.00 | 52.00 | 15.95 | 64.00 |

**DBH2**
**MR. APPLE™**

Designer: Harry Sales
Modeller: David Lyttleton
Height: 3 1/4", 8.3 cm
Colour: Black trousers, white and blue striped shirt, white apron
Issued: 1982 to the present

Royal Doulton
MR APPLE

| *Back Stamp* | *U.S. $* | *Price Can. $* | *U.K. £* | *Aust. $* |
|---|---|---|---|---|
| BH-1 | 40.00 | 52.00 | 14.95 | 64.00 |

**DBH3**
**MRS. APPLE™**

Designer: Harry Sales
Modeller: David Lyttleton
Height: 3 1/4", 8.3 cm
Colour: White and blue striped dress, white apron
Issued: 1982 to the present

Royal Doulton
MRS. APPLE

| *Back Stamp* | *U.S. $* | *Price Can. $* | *U.K. £* | *Aust. $* |
|---|---|---|---|---|
| BH-1 | 40.00 | 52.00 | 14.95 | 64.00 |

**DBH4**
**LORD WOODHOUSE™**

| | |
|---|---|
| Designer: | Harry Sales |
| Modeller: | David Lyttleton |
| Height: | 3 1/4", 8.3 cm |
| Colour: | Green trousers, brown coat and burgundy waistcoat |
| Issued: | 1982 to the present |

| *Back Stamp* | *U.S. $* | *Price Can. $* | *U.K. £* | *Aust. $* |
|---|---|---|---|---|
| BH-1 | 40.00 | 52.00 | 15.95 | 64.00 |

**DBH5**
**LADY WOODMOUSE™**

| | |
|---|---|
| Designer: | Harry Sales |
| Modeller: | David Lyttleton |
| Height: | 3 1/4", 8.3 cm |
| Colour: | Red and white striped dress, white apron |
| Issued: | 1982 to the present |

| *Back Stamp* | *U.S. $* | *Price Can. $* | *U.K. £* | *Aust. $* |
|---|---|---|---|---|
| BH-1 | 25.00 | 52.00 | 15.95 | 64.00 |

**DBH6**
**DUSTY DOGWOOD™**

| | |
|---|---|
| Designer: | Harry Sales |
| Modeller: | David Lyttleton |
| Height: | 3 1/4", 8.3 cm |
| Colour: | Dark grey suit, red waistcoat |
| Issued: | 1982 to the present |

| *Back Stamp* | *U.S. $* | *Price Can. $* | *U.K. £* | *Aust. $* |
|---|---|---|---|---|
| BH-1 | 40.00 | 52.00 | 14.95 | 64.00 |

**DBH7**
**WILFRID TOADFLAX™**

| | |
|---|---|
| Designer: | Harry Sales |
| Modeller: | David Lyttleton |
| Height: | 3 1/4", 8.3 cm |
| Colour: | Grey trousers, red and white striped shirt |
| Issued: | 1982 to the present |

Royal Doulton
WILFRED TOADFLAX
DBH 7
FROM THE BRAMBLY HEDGE
GIFT COLLECTION
© JILL BARKLEM 1982

| *Back Stamp* | *U.S. $* | *Price Can. $* | *U.K. £* | *Aust. $* |
|---|---|---|---|---|
| BH-1 | 38.00 | 52.00 | 14.95 | 60.00 |

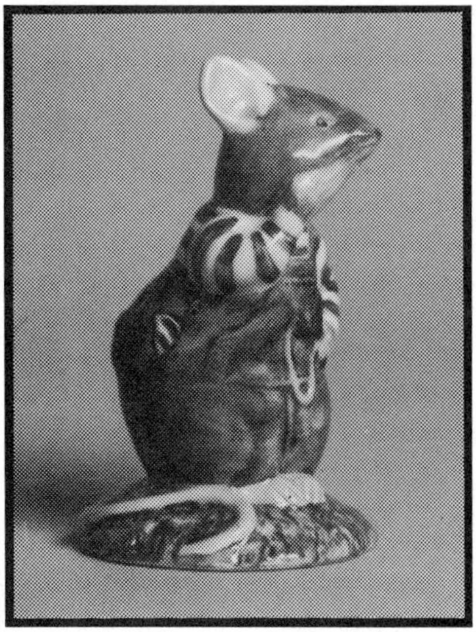

**DBH8**
**PRIMROSE WOODMOUSE™**

| | |
|---|---|
| Designer: | Harry Sales |
| Modeller: | David Lyttleton |
| Height: | 3 1/4", 8.3 cm |
| Colour: | Yellow dress with white apron |
| Issued: | 1982 to the present |

Royal Doulton
PRIMROSE WOODMOUSE
DBH 8
FROM THE BRAMBLY HEDGE
GIFT COLLECTION
© JILL BARKLEM 1982

| *Back Stamp* | *U.S. $* | *Price Can. $* | *U.K. £* | *Aust. $* |
|---|---|---|---|---|
| BH-1 | 38.00 | 52.00 | 14.95 | 60.00 |

**DBH9**
**OLD MRS. EYEBRIGHT™**

| | |
|---|---|
| Designer: | Harry Sales |
| Modeller: | David Lyttleton |
| Height: | 3 1/4, 8.3 cm" |
| Colour: | Mauve skirt, white and pink striped shawl, white apron |
| Issued: | 1983 to the present |

Royal Doulton
OLD MRS EYEBRIGHT
DBH 9
FROM THE BRAMBLY HEDGE
GIFT COLLECTION
© JILL BARKLEM 1983

| *Back Stamp* | *U.S. $* | *Price Can. $* | *U.K. £* | *Aust. $* |
|---|---|---|---|---|
| BH-1 | 40.00 | 52.00 | 15.95 | 64.00 |

## DBH10
## MR. TOADFLAX™

| | |
|---|---|
| Designer: | Harry Sales |
| Modeller: | David Lyttleton |
| Height: | 3 1/4", 8.3 cm |
| Colour: | Blue and white striped shirt, pink trousers |
| Issued: | 1983 to the present |

Royal Doulton
MR. TOADFLAX
DBH 10
FROM THE BRAMBLY HEDGE
GIFT COLLECTION
© JILL BARKLEM 1983

| *Back Stamp* | *U.S. $* | *Price Can. $* | *U.K. £* | *Aust. $* |
|---|---|---|---|---|
| BH-1 | 40.00 | 52.00 | 15.95 | 64.00 |

## DBH11
## MRS. TOADFLAX™

| | |
|---|---|
| Designer: | Harry Sales |
| Modeller: | David Lyttleton |
| Height: | 3 1/4", 8.3 cm |
| Colour: | Green and white striped dress, white apron |
| Issued: | 1985 to the present |

Royal Doulton®
MRS TOADFLAX
DBH 11
FROM THE BRAMBLY HEDGE
GIFT COLLECTION
© 1985 JILL BARKLEM

| *Back Stamp* | *U.S. $* | *Price Can. $* | *U.K. £* | *Aust. $* |
|---|---|---|---|---|
| BH-1 | 40.00 | 52.00 | 15.95 | 64.00 |

## DBH12
## CATKIN™

| | |
|---|---|
| Designer: | Harry Sales |
| Modeller: | David Lyttleton |
| Height: | 3 1/4", 8.3 cm |
| Colour: | Yellow dress with white apron |
| Issued: | 1985 to the present |

| *Back Stamp* | *U.S. $* | *Price Can. $* | *U.K. £* | *Aust. $* |
|---|---|---|---|---|
| BH-1 | 34.00 | 52.00 | 14.95 | 54.00 |

**DBH13**
**OLD VOLE™**

Designer: Harry Sales
Modeller: David Lyttleton
Height: 3 1/4", 8.3 cm
Colour: Green jacket,blue trousers, yellow waistcoar
Issued: 1985 - 1992

Royal Doulton®
OLD VOLE
D.B.H. 13
FROM THE BRAMBLY HEDGE
GIFT COLLECTION
© 1985 JILL BARKLEM

| Back Stamp | U.S. $ | Price Can. $ | U.K. £ | Aust. $ |
|---|---|---|---|---|
| BH-1 | 75.00 | 100.00 | 35.00 | 75.00 |

**DBH14**
**BASIL™**

Designer: Harry Sales
Modeller: David Lyttleton
Height: 3 1/4", 8.3 cm
Colour: Brown waistcoat, green and white striped trousers
Issued: 1985 - 1992

Royal Doulton®
BASIL

| Back Stamp | U.S. $ | Price Can. $ | U.K. £ | Aust. $ |
|---|---|---|---|---|
| BH-1 | 75.00 | 100.00 | 35.00 | 70.00 |

**DBH15**
**MRS. CRUSTYBREAD™**

Designer: Graham Tongue
Modeller: Ted Chawner
Height: 3 1/4", 8.3 cm
Colour: Yellow dress, white apron and cap
Issued: 1987 to the present

Royal Doulton®
MRS. CRUSTYBREAD

| Back Stamp | U.S. $ | Price Can. $ | U.K. £ | Aust. $ |
|---|---|---|---|---|
| BH-1 | 34.00 | 52.00 | 14.95 | 54.00 |

**DBH16**
**CLOVER™**

Designer: Graham Tongue
Modeller: Graham Tongue
Height: 3 1/4", 8.3 cm
Colour: Burgundy dress, white apron
Issued: 1987 to the present

Royal Doulton®
CLOVER
DBH 16
FROM THE BRAMBLY HEDGE
GIFT COLLECTION
© 1987 JILL BARKLEM

| *Back Stamp* | *U.S. $* | *Price Can. $* | *U.K. £* | *Aust. $* |
|---|---|---|---|---|
| BH-1 | 34.00 | 52.00 | 14.95 | 54.00 |

**DBH17**
**TEASEL™**

Designer: Graham Tongue
Modeller: Ted Chawner
Height: 3 1/4", 8.3 cm
Colour: Blue-grey dungarees, blue and white striped shirt
Issued: 1987 - 1993

Royal Doulton®
TEASEL
DBH 17
FROM THE BRAMBLY HEDGE
GIFT COLLECTION
© 1987 JILL BARKLEM

| *Back Stamp* | *U.S. $* | *Price Can. $* | *U.K. £* | *Aust. $* |
|---|---|---|---|---|
| BH-1 | 75.00 | 100.00 | 35.00 | 54.00 |

**DBH18**
**STORE STUMP MONEY BOX™**

Designer: Martyn Alcock
Height: 3 1/4", 8.3 cm
Colour: Brown
Issued: 1987 to the present

Royal Doulton®
STORE STUMP MONEY BOX
DBH 18
FROM THE BRAMBLY HEDGE
GIFT COLLECTION
© 1987 JILL BARKLEM

| *Back Stamp* | *U.S. $* | *Price Can. $* | *U.K. £* | *Aust. $* |
|---|---|---|---|---|
| BH-1 | 75.00 | 100.00 | 30.00 | 50.00 |

## DBH19
## LILY WEAVER™

| | |
|---|---|
| Designer: | Graham Tongue |
| Modeller: | Ted Chawner |
| Height: | 3 1/4", 8.3 cm |
| Colour: | White dress with green and mauve, white cap |
| Issued: | 1988 - 1993 |

| *Back Stamp* | *U.S. $* | *Price Can. $* | *U.K. £* | *Aust. $* |
|---|---|---|---|---|
| BH-1 | 22.50 | 40.00 | 20.00 | 62.00 |

## DBH20
## FLAX WEAVER™

| | |
|---|---|
| Designer: | Graham Tongue |
| Modeller: | Ted Chawner |
| Height: | 3 1/4", 8.3 cm |
| Colour: | Grey trousers, grey and white striped shirt |
| Issued: | 1988 - 1993 |

| *Back Stamp:* | *U.S. $* | *Price Can. $* | *U.K. £* | *Aust. $* |
|---|---|---|---|---|
| BH-1 | 22.50 | 40.00 | 20.00 | 60.00 |

## DBH21
## CONKER™

| | |
|---|---|
| Designer: | Graham Tongue |
| Modeller: | Ted Chawner |
| Height: | 3 1/4", 8.3 cm |
| Colour: | Green jacket, yellow waistcoat, green striped trousers |
| Issued: | 1988 to the present |

| *Back Stamp* | *U.S. $* | *Price Can. $* | *U.K. £* | *Aust. $* |
|---|---|---|---|---|
| BH-1 | 40.00 | 52.00 | 15.95 | 64.00 |

**DBH22**
**PRIMROSE ENTERTAINS™**

| | |
|---|---|
| Designer: | Graham Tongue |
| Modeller: | Alan Maslankowski |
| Height: | 3 1/4", 8.3 cm |
| Colour: | Green and yellow dress |
| Issued: | 1991 to the present |

| *Back Stamp* | *U.S. $* | *Price Can. $* | *U.K. £* | *Aust. $* |
|---|---|---|---|---|
| BH-1 | 66.00 | 96.00 | 24.00 | 100.00 |

**DBH23**
**WILFRID ENTERTAINS™**

| | |
|---|---|
| Designer: | Graham Tongue |
| Modeller: | Alan Maslankowski |
| Height: | 3 1/4", 8.3 cm |
| Colour: | Burgundy and yellow outfit, black hat |
| Issued: | 1991 to the present |

| *Back Stamp* | *U.S. $* | *Price Can. $* | *U.K. £* | *Aust $* |
|---|---|---|---|---|
| BH-1 | 66.00 | 96.00 | 24.00 | 109.00 |

**DBH24**
**MR. SALTAPPLE™**

| | |
|---|---|
| Designer: | Graham Tongue |
| Modeller: | Warren Platt |
| Height: | 3 1/4", 8.3 cm |
| Colour: | Blue and white striped outfit, beige base |
| Issued: | 1993 to the present |

| *Back Stamp* | *U.S. $* | *Price Can. $* | *U.K. £* | *Aust. $* |
|---|---|---|---|---|
| BH-1 | 40.00 | 52.00 | 15.95 | 79.00 |

**DBH25**
**MRS. SALTAPPLE™**

| | |
|---|---|
| Designer: | Graham Tongue |
| Modeller: | Warren Platt |
| Height: | 3 1/4", 8.3 cm |
| Colour: | Rose and cream dress, beige hat and base |
| Issued: | 1993 to the present |

Royal Doulton®
MRS. SALTAPPLE

| *Back Stamp* | *U.S. $* | *Price Can. $* | *U.K. £* | *Aust. $* |
|---|---|---|---|---|
| BH-1 | 40.00 | 52.00 | 15.95 | 79.00 |

ROYAL DOULTON
BUNNYKINS

# *BUNNYKINS*

# BUNNYKINS BACKSTAMPS

## BK-1. DOULTON & CO. LIMITED: 1972-1976

Used on all figurines introduced between 1972 and 1976.

## BK-2. ROYAL DOULTON TABLEWARE LTD: 1976-1984

The "Doulton & Co. Limited" was changed to "Royal Doulton Tableware Ltd." Used on all new figurines introduced between 1976 and 1984. This new backstamp was also on all models that had been in production previously updating the older backstamp (BK-1). In these instances the copyright year on the stamps was kept the same as that of the original backstamp (BK-1).

## BK-3 GOLDEN JUBILEE CELEBRATION: 1984

All Models manufactured during 1984 carried the words Golden Jubilee Celebration 1984 which was added to the 1976-1984 backstamp (BK-2).

## BK-4. ROYAL DOULTON (U.K.): 1985-1986

The backstamp of 1976-1984 was modified to "Royal Doulton (U.K.)". All items introduced between 1985 and 1986 carry this backstamp.

## BK-5. ROYAL DOULTON: 1987 TO DATE

The backstamp of 1985-86 was again modified by removing the (U.K.). All new figurines introduced since 1987 carry this backstamp.

## BK-SPECIALS. SPECIAL COMMISSION

Many figurines are issued for special events, anniversaries, promotions etc. All these carry a special stamp.

D6003
D6004
D6002
D6025
D6001
D6024

JEMIMA PUDDLE-DUCK™
Large Size | Wall Plaque | Gold Backstamp | Character Jug

DISPLAY STAND
Pig-Wig™ | Simpkin™ | Duchess™ | Ginger™ | Amiable Guinea Pig™

TIMMY TIPTOES™
**First Version** **Second Version**

SQUIRREL NUTKIN™
**First Version** **Second Version**

TOM KITTEN™
**First Version** **Second Version**

PETER RABBIT™
**First Version** **Second Version**

APPLEY DAPPLY™ — First Version, Second Version
MRS. TIGGY WINKLE™ — First Version, Second Version on a Tree Lamp Base

TOMMY BROCK™ — Spade Out, Spade In
MR. BENJAMIN BUNNY™ — First Version, Second Version

MISS MOPPET™
**First Version** **Second Version**

TABITHA TWITCHIT™
**First Version** **Second Version**

LITTLE PIG ROBINSON™
**First Version** **Second Version**

PIGLING BLAND™
**First Version** **Second Version**

FIERCE BAD RABBIT™
First Version Second Version

BENJAMIN BUNNY SAT ON A BANK™
First Version Second Version

MR. JEREMY FISHER™
First Version Second Version

MR. JACKSON™
First Version Second Version

BENJAMIN BUNNY™

First Version | Second Version | Third Version

MRS. RABBIT™

First Version | Second Version

CECILEY PARSLEY™

First Version | Second Version

TOM KITTEN™
Character Jug　Large Size　First Version　Second Version

PETER RABBIT™
Large Size　First Version　Second Version　Character Jug

TOMMY BROCK™

First Version Second Version Third Version Fourth Version

DUCHESS™

Style Two Style One

**BILLY BUNNYKINS™**
**D6001**

Designer: Charles Noke
Height: 4 1/2", 11.4 cm
Colour: Brown bunny, red trousers blue jacket, white bow tie with blue spots
Issued: 1939-c.1940's

**FARMER BUNNYKINS™**
**D6003**

Designer: Charles Noke
Height: 7 1/2", 19 cm
Colour: Green, blue, brown, red and white
Issued: 1939-c.1940's

**FREDDIE BUNNYKINS™**
**D6024**

Designer: Charles Noke
Height: 3 3/4", 9.5 cm
Colour: Brown bunny, Green trousers red jacket and yellow bow tie
Issued: 1939-c.1940's

**MARY BUNNYKINS™**
**D6002**

Designer: Charles Noke
Height: 6 1/2", 16.5 cm
Colour: Brown bunny, blue and red dress with white apron
Issued: 1939-c.1940's

**MOTHER BUNNYKINS™**
**D6004**

Designer: Charles Noke
Height: 7", 17.5 cm
Colour: Blue, red, white and brown
Issued: 1939-c.1940's

**REGGIE BUNNYKINS™**
**D6004**

Designer: Charles Noke
Height: 3 3/4", 9.5 cm
Colour: Brown bunny, blue dress and red bow tie
Issued: 1939-c.1940's

| *Name* | *Back Stamp* | *Doulton Number* | *Price U.S. $* | *Can. $* | *U.K. £* | *Aust. $* |
|---|---|---|---|---|---|---|
| Billy Bunnykins | BK- | D6001 | 2,800.00 | 3,000.00 | 850.00 | 3,000.00 |
| Farmer Bunnykins | BK- | D6003 | 3,300.00 | 3,500.00 | 1,800.00 | 3,500.00 |
| Freddie Bunnykins | BK- | D6024 | 3,300.00 | 3,500.00 | 1,800.00 | 3,500.00 |
| Mary Bunnykins | BK- | D6002 | 3,000.00 | 3,200.00 | 1,500.00 | 3,200.00 |
| Mother Bunnykins | BK- | D6004 | 3,300.00 | 3,500.00 | 1,800.00 | 3,500.00 |
| Reggie Bunnykins | BK- | D6025 | 3,300.00 | 3,500.00 | 1,800.00 | 3,500.00 |

**D6615A**
**BUNNY BANK™**
**First Version**

| | |
|---|---|
| Designer: | Unknown |
| Modeller: | Unknown |
| Height: | 8 1/2", 21.6 cm |
| Colour: | Grey rabbit, green coat and hat, maroon drum |
| Issued: | 1967 - 1977 |

| Back Stamp | U.S. $ | Price Can. $ | U.K. £ | Aust. $ |
|---|---|---|---|---|
| BK- | 250.00 | 300.00 | 150.00 | 325.00 |

**D6615B**
**BUNNY BANK™**
**Second Version**

| | |
|---|---|
| Designer: | Unknown |
| Modeller: | Unknown |
| Height: | 9 1/4", 23.5 cm |
| Colour: | Brown rabbit, green coat and hat, maroon drum |
| Issued: | 1979 - 1991 |

MADE IN ENGLAND ROYAL DOULTON ENGLAND
Bunnybank
D.6615
© DOULTON & CO.LIMITED 1967

| *Back Stamp* | *U.S. $* | *Price Can. $* | *U.K. £* | *Aust. $* |
|---|---|---|---|---|
| BK- | 150.00 | 200.00 | 100.00 | 225.00 |

**DB1**
**FAMILY PHOTOGRAPH BUNNYKINS ™**
**First Version**

| | |
|---|---|
| Designer: | Walter Hayward |
| Modeller: | Albert Hallam |
| Height: | 4 1/2", 11.4 cm |
| Colour: | Blue, white, burgundy and grey |
| Issued: | 1972 - 1988 (© 1972) |
| Varieties: | DB67 |

| *Back Stamp* | *U.S. $* | *Price Can. $* | *U.K. £* | *Aust. $* |
|---|---|---|---|---|
| BK-1 | 85.00 | 135.00 | 55.00 | 90.00 |
| BK-2 | 85.00 | 135.00 | 55.00 | 90.00 |
| BK-3 | 85.00 | 135.00 | 55.00 | 90.00 |

**DB2**
**BUNTIE BUNNYKINS HELPING MOTHER™**

| | |
|---|---|
| Designer: | Walter Hayward |
| Modeller: | Albert Hallam |
| Height: | 3 1/2", 8.9 cm |
| Colour: | Rose-pink and yellow |
| Issued: | 1972 - 1993 (© 1972) |

| *Back Stamp* | *U.S. $* | *Price Can. $* | *U.K. £* | *Aust. $* |
|---|---|---|---|---|
| BK-1 | 50.00 | 60.00 | 25.00 | 57.00 |
| BK-2 | 50.00 | 60.00 | 25.00 | 57.00 |
| BK-3 | 50.00 | 60.00 | 25.00 | 57.00 |

**DB3**
**BILLIE BUNNYKINS COOLING OFF™**

| | |
|---|---|
| Designer: | Walter Hayward |
| Modeller: | Albert Hallam |
| Height: | 3 3/4", 9.5 cm |
| Colour: | Burgundy, yellow and green-grey |
| Issued: | 1972 - 1987 (© 1972) |

| *Back Stamp* | *U.S. $* | *Price Can. $* | *U.K. £* | *Aust. $* |
|---|---|---|---|---|
| BK-1 | 150.00 | 175.00 | 150.00 | 100.00 |
| BK-2 | 150.00 | 175.00 | 150.00 | 100.00 |
| BK-3 | 150.00 | 175.00 | 150.00 | 100.00 |

**DB4**
**BILLIE AND BUNTIE BUNNYKINS SLEIGH RIDE™**
**First Version**

Designer: Walter Hayward
Modeller: Albert Hallam
Height: 3 1/4", 8.3 cm
Colour: Blue, maroon and yellow
Issued: 1972 to the present (© 1972)
Varieties: DB81

MADE IN ENGLAND ROYAL DOULTON ENGLAND
BILLIE & BUNTIE BUNNYKINS
"Sleigh Ride"
DB4
© ROYAL DOULTON TABLEWARE LTD 1972

| *Back Stamp* | *U.S. $* | *Price Can. $* | *U.K. £* | *Aust. $* |
|---|---|---|---|---|
| BK-1 | 40.00 | 45.00 | 13.50 | 59.00 |
| BK-2 | 40.00 | 45.00 | 13.50 | 59.00 |
| BK-3 | 40.00 | 45.00 | 13.50 | 59.00 |

**DB5**
**MR. BUNNYKINS AUTUMN DAYS™**

Designer: Walter Hayward
Modeller: Albert Hallam
Height: 4', 10.1 cm
Colour: Maroon, yellow and blue
Issued: 1972 - 1982 (© 1972)

MR. BUNNYKINS
Autumn Days
DB5
COPR 1972
DOULTON & CO LIMITED
Rd No 956236
Rd No 12903
R.S.A Rd No 192/72

| *Back Stamp* | *U.S. $* | *Price Can. $* | *U.K. £* | *Aust. $* |
|---|---|---|---|---|
| BK-1 | 375.00 | 400.00 | 225.00 | 300.00 |
| BK-2 | 375.00 | 400.00 | 225.00 | 300.00 |
| BK-3 | 375.00 | 400.00 | 225.00 | 300.00 |

**DB6**
**MRS. BUNNYKINS CLEAN SWEEP™**

Designer: Walter Hayward
Modeller: Albert Hallam
Height: 4", 10.1 cm
Colour: Blue and white
Issued: 1972 - 1991 (© 1972)

MRS. BUNNYKINS
"Clean Sweep"
DB6
COPR 1972
DOULTON & CO LIMITED
Rd No 956233
Rd No 12904
R S A Rd No 186/72

| *Back Stamp* | *U.S. $* | *Price Can. $* | *U.K. £* | *Aust. $* |
|---|---|---|---|---|
| BK-1 | 45.00 | 50.00 | 13.00 | 64.00 |
| BK-2 | 45.00 | 50.00 | 13.00 | 64.00 |
| BK-3 | 45.00 | 50.00 | 13.00 | 64.00 |
| BK-6 | 45.00 | 50.00 | 13.00 | 64.00 |

## DB7
## DAISIE BUNNYKINS SPRINGTIME™

Designer: Walter Hayward
Modeller: Albert Hallam
Height: 3 1/2", 8.9 cm
Colour: Blue, white and yellow
Issued: 1972 - 1983 (© 1972)

| *Back Stamp* | *U.S. $* | *Price Can.* | *U.K. £* | *Aust. $* |
|---|---|---|---|---|
| BK-1 | 425.00 | 450.00 | 275.00 | 375.00 |
| BK-2 | 425.00 | 450.00 | 275.00 | 375.00 |
| BK-3 | 425.00 | 450.00 | 275.00 | 375.00 |

## DB8
## DOLLIE BUNNYKINS PLAYTIME™

Designer: Walter Hayward
Modeller: Albert Hallam
Height: 4", 10.1 cm
Colour: White dress with pink design; blue dress
Issued: 1972 - 1993 (© 1972)
Varieties: DB80

| *Back Stamp* | *U.S. $* | *Price Can. $* | *U.K. £* | *Aust. $* |
|---|---|---|---|---|
| BK-1 | 45.00 | 50.00 | 23.00 | 64.00 |
| BK-2 | 45.00 | 50.00 | 23.00 | 64.00 |
| BK-3 | 45.00 | 50.00 | 23.00 | 64.00 |

## DB9
## STORYTIME BUNNYKINS™
**First Version**

Designer: Walter Hayward
Modeller: Albert Hallam
Height: 3", 7.6 cm
Colour: White dress with blue design; pink dress
Issued: 1972 to the present (© 1972)
Varieties: DB59

| *Back Stamp* | *U.S. $* | *Price Can. $* | *U.K. £* | *Aust. $* |
|---|---|---|---|---|
| BK-1 | 35.00 | 45.00 | 13.50 | 64.00 |
| BK-2 | 35.00 | 45.00 | 13.50 | 64.00 |
| BK-3 | 35.00 | 45.00 | 13.50 | 64.00 |

**DB10**
**BUSY NEEDLES BUNNYKINS™**

| | |
|---|---|
| Designer: | Walter Hayward |
| Modeller: | Albert Hallam |
| Height: | 3 1/4", 8.3 cm |
| Colour: | White, green and maroon |
| Issued: | 1973 - 1988 (©1974) |
| Varieties: | DB70 |

| *Back* | | *Price* | | |
|---|---|---|---|---|
| *Stamp* | *U.S. $* | *Can. $* | *U.K. £* | *Aust. $* |
| BK-1 | 65.00 | 85.00 | 55.00 | 95.00 |
| BK-2 | 65.00 | 85.00 | 55.00 | 95.00 |
| BK-3 | 65.00 | 85.00 | 55.00 | 95.00 |

**DB11**
**RISE AND SHINE BUNNYKINS™**

| | |
|---|---|
| Designer: | Walter Hayward |
| Modeller: | Albert Hallam |
| Height: | 3 3/4", 9.5 cm |
| Colour: | Maroon, yellow and blue |
| Issued: | 1973 - 1988 (© 1974) |

| *Back* | | *Price* | | |
|---|---|---|---|---|
| *Stamp* | *U.S. $* | *Can. $* | *U.K. £* | *Aust. $* |
| BK-1 | 125.00 | 150.00 | 95.00 | 95.00 |
| BK-2 | 125.00 | 150.00 | 95.00 | 95.00 |
| BK-3 | 125.00 | 150.00 | 95.00 | 95.00 |

**DB12**
**TALLY HO! BUNNYKINS ™**
**First Version**

| | |
|---|---|
| Designer: | Walter Hayward |
| Modeller: | Albert Hallam |
| Height: | 3 3/4", 9.5 cm |
| Colour: | Burgundy, yellow, blue, white and green |
| Issued: | 1973 - 1988 |
| Varieties: | DB78 (© 1974) |

| *Back* | | *Price* | | |
|---|---|---|---|---|
| *Stamp* | *U.S. $* | *Can. $* | *U.K. £* | *Aust. $* |
| BK-1 | 75.00 | 115.00 | 45.00 | 70.00 |
| BK-2 | 75.00 | 115.00 | 45.00 | 70.00 |
| BK-3 | 75.00 | 115.00 | 45.00 | 70.00 |

**DB13**
**THE ARTIST™**

Designer: Walter Hayward
Modeller: Alan Maslankowski
Height: 3 3/4", 9.5 cm
Colour: Burgundy, yellow and blue
Issued: 1974 - 1982 (© 1975)

BUNNYKINS ®
The Artist
DB 13
© ROYAL DOULTON
TABLEWARE LTD 1975

| *Back Stamp* | *U.S. $* | *Price Can. $* | *U.K. £* | *Aust. $* |
|---|---|---|---|---|
| BK-1 | 400.00 | 450.00 | 250.00 | 300.00 |
| BK-2 | 400.00 | 450.00 | 250.00 | 300.00 |

**DB14**
**GRANDPA'S STORY BUNNYKINS™**

Designer: Walter Hayward
Modeller: Alan Maslankowski
Height: 4", 10.1 cm
Colour: Burgundy, grey, yellow, blue and green
Issued: 1974 - 1983 (© 1975)

BUNNYKINS
Grandpa's Story
DB 14
© ROYAL DOULTON
TABLEWARE LTD 1975

| *Back Stamp* | *U.S. $* | *Price Can. $* | *U.K. £* | *Aust. $* |
|---|---|---|---|---|
| BK-1 | 350.00 | 400.00 | 250.00 | 350.00 |
| BK-2 | 350.00 | 400.00 | 250.00 | 350.00 |

**DB15**
**SLEEPYTIME™**

Designer: Walter Hayward
Modeller: Alan Maslankowski
Height: 1 3/4", 4.7 cm
Colour: Brown, white, yellow, blue and red
Issued: 1974 - 1993 (© 1975)

BUNNYKINS ®
Sleepytime
DB 15
© ROYAL DOULTON
TABLEWARE LTD 1975

| *Back Stamp* | *U.S. $* | *Price Can. $* | *U.K. £* | *Aust. $* |
|---|---|---|---|---|
| BK-1 | 50.00 | 50.00 | 20.00 | 57.00 |
| BK-2 | 50.00 | 50.00 | 20.00 | 57.00 |
| BK-3 | 50.00 | 50.00 | 20.00 | 57.00 |

**DB16**
**MR. BUNNYBEAT STRUMMING™**

| | |
|---|---|
| Designer: | Harry Sales |
| Modeller: | David Lyttleton |
| Height: | 4 1/2", 11.4 cm |
| Colour: | Pink and yellow coat, blue and white striped trousers, white with blue polka-dot neck-bow |
| Issued: | 1982 - 1988 (© 1981) |

MADE IN ENGLAND ROYAL DOULTON ENGLAND
MR. BUNNYBEAT
Strumming
DB 16
© ROYAL DOULTON
TABLEWARE LTD 1981

| *Back Stamp* | *U.S. $* | *Price Can. $* | *U.K. £* | *Aust. $* |
|---|---|---|---|---|
| BK-2 | 100.00 | 125.00 | 75.00 | 90.00 |
| BK-3 | 100.00 | 125.00 | 75.00 | 90.00 |

**DB17**
**SANTA BUNNYKINS HAPPY CHRISTMAS™**

| | |
|---|---|
| Designer: | Harry Sales |
| Modeller: | David Lyttleton |
| Height: | 4 1/2", 10.8 cm |
| Colour: | Red, white and brown |
| Issued: | 1981 to the present (© 1981) |

MADE IN ENGLAND ROYAL DOULTON ENGLAND
SANTA BUNNYKINS
Happy Christmas
DB 17
© ROYAL DOULTON
TABLEWARE LTD 1981

| *Back Stamp* | *U.S. $* | *Price Can. $* | *U.K. £* | *Aust. $* |
|---|---|---|---|---|
| BK-2 | 40.00 | 52.00 | 16.95 | 64.00 |
| BK-3 | 40.00 | 52.00 | 16.95 | 64.00 |

**DB18**
**MR. BUNNYKINS AT THE EASTER PARADE ™**
**First Version**

| | |
|---|---|
| Designer: | Harry Sales |
| Modeller: | David Littleton |
| Height: | 5", 12.7 cm |
| Colour: | Red, yellow and brown |
| Issued: | 1982 - 1993 (© 1982) |
| Varieties: | DB 51 |

MADE IN ENGLAND ROYAL DOULTON ENGLAND
MR BUNNYKINS
At The Easter Parade
DB 18
© ROYAL DOULTON
TABLEWARE LTD 1982

| *Back Stamp* | *U.S. $* | *Price Can. $* | *U.K. £* | *Aust. $* |
|---|---|---|---|---|
| BK-2 | 50.00 | 70.00 | 20.00 | 80.00 |
| BK-3 | 50.00 | 70.00 | 20.00 | 80.00 |

**DB19**
**MRS. BUNNYKINS AT THE EASTER PARADE ™**
**First Version**

| | |
|---|---|
| Designer: | Harry Sales |
| Modeller: | David Lyttleton |
| Height: | 4 1/2", 11.4 cm |
| Colour: | Pale blue and maroon |
| Issued: | 1982 to the present (© 1982) |
| Varieties: | DB 52 |

MRS BUNNYKINS
At The Easter Parade
DB 19
© ROYAL DOULTON
TABLEWARE LTD 1982

| *Back Stamp* | *U.S. $* | *Price Can. $* | *U.K. £* | *Aust. $* |
|---|---|---|---|---|
| BK-2 | 40.00 | 52.00 | 16.95 | 80.00 |
| BK-3 | 40.00 | 52.00 | 16.95 | 80.00 |

**DB20**
**ASTRO BUNNYKINS ROCKET MAN™**

| | |
|---|---|
| Designer: | Harry Sales |
| Modeller: | David Lyttleton |
| Height: | 4 1/4", 10.8 cm |
| Colour: | White, red, blue and yellow |
| Issued: | 1983 - 1988 (© 1982) |

ASTRO BUNNYKINS
Rocket Man
DB 20
ROYAL DOULTON
TABLEWARE LTD 1982

| *Back Stamp* | *U.S. $* | *Price Can. $* | *U.K. £* | *Aust. $* |
|---|---|---|---|---|
| BK-2 | 100.00 | 125.00 | 45.00 | 85.00 |
| BK-3 | 100.00 | 125.00 | 45.00 | 85.00 |

**DB21**
**HAPPY BIRTHDAY BUNNYKINS™**

| | |
|---|---|
| Designer: | Harry Sales |
| Modeller: | Graham Tongue |
| Height: | 3 3/4", 9.5 cm |
| Colour: | Red and blue |
| Issued: | 1983 to the present (© 1982) |

BIRTHDAY BUNNYKINS"
DB 21
© ROYAL DOULTON
TABLEWARE LTD. 1982

| *Back Stamp* | *U.S. $* | *Price Can. $* | *U.K. £* | *Aust. $* |
|---|---|---|---|---|
| BK-2 | 40.00 | 52.00 | 16.95 | 70.00 |
| BK-3 | 40.00 | 52.00 | 16.95 | 70.00 |

**DB22**
**JOGGING BUNNYKINS™**

| | |
|---|---|
| Designer: | Harry Sales |
| Modeller: | David Lyttleton |
| Height: | 2 1/2", 6.4 cm |
| Colour: | Yellow, blue and white |
| Issued: | 1983 - 1989 (© 1982) |

"JOGGING BUNNYKINS"
DB22
© ROYAL DOULTON
TABLEWARE LTD 1982

| *Back Stamp* | *U.S. $* | *Price Can. $* | *U.K. £* | *Aust. $* |
|---|---|---|---|---|
| BK-2 | 75.00 | 100.00 | 55.00 | 90.00 |
| BK-3 | 75.00 | 100.00 | 55.00 | 90.00 |

**DB23**
**SOUSAPHONE BUNNYKINS ™**
**First Version**

| | |
|---|---|
| Designer: | Harry Sales |
| Modeller: | David Lyttleton |
| Height: | 3 1/2", 8.9 cm |
| Colour: | Red, blue and yellow |
| Issued: | 1984 - 1990 (© 1983) |
| Varieties: | DB86, DB105 |
| Series: | Bunnykins Oompah Band / **"Bunnykins Oompah Band To Celebrate Bunnykins 50th Anniversary 1984 on DB 23 to DB 27 ???** |

"SOUSAPHONE BUNNYKINS"
FROM THE OOMPAH BAND
DB 23
© ROYAL DOULTON
TABLEWARE LTD. 1983
GOLDEN JUBILEE
CELEBRATION 1984

| *Back Stamp* | *U.S. $* | *Price Can. $* | *U.K. £* | *Aust. $* |
|---|---|---|---|---|
| BK-3 | 95.00 | 100.00 | 30.00 | 95.00 |

**DB24**
**TRUMPETER BUNNYKINS™**
**First Version**

| | |
|---|---|
| Designer: | Harry Sales |
| Modeller: | David Lyttleton |
| Height: | 3 1/2', 8.9 cm |
| Colour: | Red, blue and yellow |
| Issued: | 1984 - 1990 |
| Varieties: | DB87, DB106 |
| Series: | Bunnykins Oompah Band |

"TRUMPETER BUNNYKINS"
FROM THE OOMPAH BAND
DB 24
© ROYAL DOULTON
TABLEWARE LTD 1983
GOLDEN JUBILEE
CELEBRATION 1984

| *Back Stamp* | *U.S. $* | *Price Can. $* | *U.K. £* | *Aust. $* |
|---|---|---|---|---|
| BK-3 | 95.00 | 100.00 | 20.00 | 95.00 |

## DB25
## CYMBALS BUNNYKINS™
**First Version**

| | |
|---|---|
| Designer: | Harry Sales |
| Modeller: | David Lyttleton |
| Height: | 3 1/2", 8.9 cm |
| Colour: | Red, blue and yellow |
| Issued: | 1984 - 1990 (© 1972) |
| Varieties: | DB 88, DB 107 |
| Series: | Bunnykins Oompah Band |

"CYMBALS BUNNYKINS"
FROM THE OOMPAH BAND
DB 25
© ROYAL DOULTON
TABLEWARE LTD. 1983
GOLDEN JUBILEE
CELEBRATION 1984

| *Back Stamp* | *U.S. $* | *Price Can. $* | *U.K. £* | *Aust. $* |
|---|---|---|---|---|
| BK-3 | 95.00 | 95.00 | 30.00 | 95.00 |

## DB26A
## DRUMMER BUNNYKINS ™
**Bunnykins Oompah Band Edition**
**First Version**

| | |
|---|---|
| Designer: | Harry Sales |
| Modeller: | David Lyttleton |
| Height: | 3 3/4", 9.5 cm |
| Colour: | Blue, yellow, red and cream |
| Issued: | 1984 - 1990 (© 1983) |
| Varieties: | DB 89, DB 108 |
| Series: | Bunnykins Oompah Band |

| *Back Stamp* | *U.S. $* | *Price Can. $* | *U.K £* | *Aust. $* |
|---|---|---|---|---|
| BK-3 | 125.00 | 100.00 | 40.00 | 110.00 |

## DB26B
## DRUMMER BUNNYKINS™
**50th Anniversary Edition**
**Second Version**

| | |
|---|---|
| Designer: | Harry Sales |
| Modeller: | David Lyttleton |
| Height: | 3 1/2", 9.2 cm |
| Colour: | Blue, yellow, red and cream |
| Issued: | 1984 - 1990 |
| Series: | Bunnykins Oompah Band |

"DRUMMER BUNNYKINS"
FROM THE OOMPAH BAND
DB 26
© ROYAL DOULTON
TABLEWARE LTD 1983
GOLDEN JUBILEE
CELEBRATION 1984

| *Back Stamp* | *U.S. $* | *Price Can. $* | *U.K. £* | *Aust. $* |
|---|---|---|---|---|
| BK-3 | 175.00 | 130.00 | 65.00 | 120.00 |

**DB27**
**DRUM-MAJOR BUNNYKINS™**
**First Version**

| | |
|---|---|
| Designer: | Harry Sales |
| Modeller: | David Lyttleton |
| Height: | 3 1/2", 8.9 cm |
| Colour: | Red, blue and yellow |
| Issued: | 1984 - 1990 |
| Varieties: | DB 90, DB 109 |
| Series: | Bunnykins Oompah Band |

DRUM-MAJOR BUNNYKINS
FROM THE OOMPAH BAND
GOLDEN JUBILEE
CELEBRATION 1984

| *Back Stamp* | *U.S. $* | *Price Can. $* | *U.K. £* | *Aust. $* |
|---|---|---|---|---|
| BK-3 | 95.00 | 95.00 | 30.00 | 95.00 |

**DB28A**
**OLYMPIC BUNNYKINS™**
**First Version**

| | |
|---|---|
| Designer: | Harry Sales |
| Modeller: | David Lyttleton |
| Height: | 3 3/4", 9.4 cm |
| Colour: | White and blue |
| Issued: | 1984 - 1988 |

"OLYMPIC BUNNYKINS"
DB28
© ROYAL DOULTON
TABLEWARE LTD 1983
GOLDEN JUBILEE
CELEBRATION 1984

| *Back Stamp* | *U.S. $* | *Price Can. $* | *U.K. £* | *Aust. $* |
|---|---|---|---|---|
| BK-3 | 95.00 | 125.00 | 35.00 | 90.00 |

**DB28B**
**OLYMPIC BUNNYKINS ™**
**Second Version**

| | |
|---|---|
| Designer: | Harry Sales |
| Modeller: | David Lyttleton |
| Height: | 3 1/2", 8.9 cm |
| Colour: | Gold and green |
| Issued: | 1984 - 1984 (© 1983) |

**Note:** Made exclusively for the Australian market.

| *Back Stamp* | *U.S. $* | *Price Can. $* | *U.K. £* | *Aust. $* |
|---|---|---|---|---|
| BK-'Special" | 195.00 | 150.00 | 75.00 | 250.00 |

**DB29A**
**TOUCHDOWN BUNNYKINS ™**
**First Version**

| | |
|---|---|
| Designer: | Harry Sales |
| Modeller: | David Lyttleton |
| Height: | 3 1/4", 8.3 cm |
| Colour: | Blue and white |
| Issued: | 1985 - 1988 |
| Varieties: | DB 96, DB 100 |

MADE IN ENGLAND ROYAL DOULTON ENGLAND
"TOUCHDOWN BUNNYKINS"
DB 29
© ROYAL DOULTON
TABLEWARE LTD 1984
GOLDEN JUBILEE
CELEBRATION 1984

| *Back Stamp* | *U.S. $* | *Price Can. $* | *U.K. £* | *Aust. $* |
|---|---|---|---|---|
| BK-4 | 75.00 | 100.00 | 55.00 | 75.00 |
| BK-5 | 75.00 | 100.00 | 55.00 | 75.00 |

*Photograph Not Available at Press Time*

**DB29B**
**TOUCHDOWN BUNNYKINS™**
**Boston College - Second Version**

| | |
|---|---|
| Designer: | Harry Sales |
| Modeller: | David Lyttleton |
| Height: | 3 1/4", 8.3 cm |
| Colour: | Maroon and gold |
| Issued: | 1985 in a limited edition of 50 |

| *Back Stamp* | *U.S. $* | *Price Can. $* | *U.K. £* | *Aust. $* |
|---|---|---|---|---|
| BK-'Special' | 1,500.00 | 1,500.00 | 750.00 | 1,500.00 |

**DB30**
**KNOCKOUT BUNNYKINS™**

| | |
|---|---|
| Designer: | Harry Sales |
| Modeller: | David Lyttleton |
| Height: | 4", 10.1 cm |
| Colour: | Yellow, green and white |
| Issued: | 1985 - 1988 © 1985 |

"KNOCKOUT BUNNYKINS"
DB 30
© ROYAL DOULTON
TABLEWARE LTD 1984

| *Back Stamp* | *U.S. $* | *Price Can. $* | *U.K. £* | *Aust. $* |
|---|---|---|---|---|
| BK-4 | 90.00 | 100.00 | 55.00 | 85.00 |
| BK-5 | 90.00 | 100.00 | 55.00 | 85.00 |

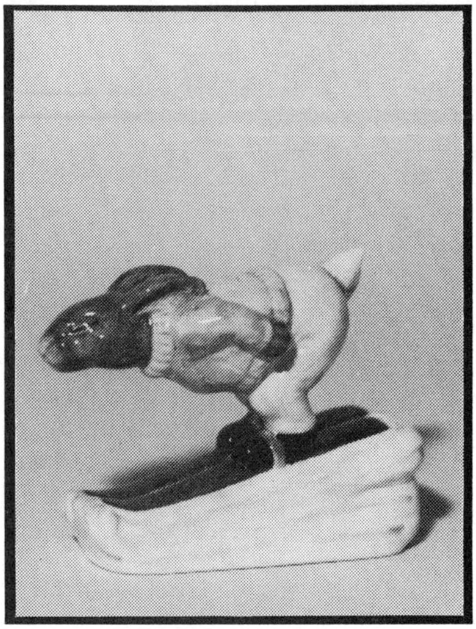

**DB31**
**DOWNHILL BUNNYKINS™**

| | |
|---|---|
| Designer: | Harry Sales |
| Modeller: | Graham Tongue |
| Height: | 2 1/2", 6.4 cm |
| Colour: | Yellow, green, maroon and grey |
| Issued: | 1985 - 1988 (© 1984) |

| *Back Stamp* | *U.S. $* | *Price Can. $* | *U.K. £* | *Aust. $* |
|---|---|---|---|---|
| BK-4 | 100.00 | 125.00 | 55.00 | 90.00 |
| BK-5 | 100.00 | 125.00 | 55.00 | 90.00 |

**DB32**
**BOGEY BUNNYKINS™**

| | |
|---|---|
| Designer: | Harry Sales |
| Modeller: | David Lyttleton |
| Height: | 4", 10.1 cm |
| Colour: | Green, brown and yellow |
| Issued: | 1985 - 1992 (© 1984) |

| *Back Stamp* | *U.S. $* | *Price Can. $* | *U.K. £* | *Aust. $* |
|---|---|---|---|---|
| BK-4 | 50.00 | 75.00 | 45.00 | 65.00 |
| BK-5 | 50.00 | 75.00 | 45.00 | 65.00 |

**DB33A**
**TALLY HO!™**
**Music Box**
**First Version**

| | |
|---|---|
| Designer: | Walter Hayward |
| Modeller: | Albert Hallam |
| Height: | 7", 17.8 cm |
| Colour: | Red coat, yellow jumper |
| Issued: | 1984 - 1993 with "Tally Ho" figurine |
| Tune: | "Rock A Bye Baby" |

| *Back Stamp* | *U.S. $* | *Price Can. $* | *U.K. £* | *Aust. $* |
|---|---|---|---|---|
| BK-4 | 75.00 | 100.00 | 55.00 | 100.00 |
| BK-5 | 75.00 | 100.00 | 55.00 | 100.00 |

**DB33B**
**TALLY HO!™**
**Music Box**
**Second Version**

| | |
|---|---|
| Designer: | Walter Hayward |
| Modeller: | Albert Hallam |
| Height: | 7", 17.8 cm |
| Colour: | Brown trousers, red coat and maroon tie |
| Issued: | 1988 - 1991 with "William" Bunnykins |
| Tune: | "Rock A Bye Baby" |

| *Back Stamp* | *U.S. $* | *Price Can. $* | *U.K. £* | *Aust. $* |
|---|---|---|---|---|
| BK-4 | 75.00 | 100.00 | 55.00 | 100.00 |
| BK-5 | 75.00 | 100.00 | 55.00 | 100.00 |

**DB34**
**SANTA BUNNYKINS™**
**Music Box**

| | |
|---|---|
| Designer: | Harry Sales |
| Modeller: | David Lyttleton |
| Height: | 7 1/4", 18.4 cm |
| Colour: | Red, white and brown |
| Issued: | 1984 - 1991 |
| Tune: | "White Christmas" |

| *Back Stamp* | *U.S. $* | *Price Can. $* | *U.K. £* | *Aust. $* |
|---|---|---|---|---|
| BK-4 | 75.00 | 100.00 | 55.00 | 100.00 |
| BK-5 | 75.00 | 100.00 | 55.00 | 100.00 |

**DB35**
**ASTRO BUNNYKINS ROCKET MAN™**
**Music Box**

| | |
|---|---|
| Designer: | Harry Sales |
| Modeller: | David Lyttleton |
| Height: | 7", 17.8 cm |
| Colour: | White, red and blue |
| Issued: | 1984 - 1989 |
| Tune: | "Fly Me To The Moon" |

| *Back Stamp* | *U.S. $* | *Price Can. $* | *U.K. £* | *Aust. $* |
|---|---|---|---|---|
| BK-4 | 125.00 | 150.00 | 75.00 | 120.00 |
| BK-5 | 125.00 | 150.00 | 75.00 | 120.00 |

**DB36**
**HAPPY BIRTHDAY BUNNYKINS™**
**Music Box**

| | |
|---|---|
| Designer: | Harry Sales |
| Modeller: | Graham Tongue |
| Height: | 7", 17.8 cm |
| Colour: | Red and white |
| Issued: | 1984 - 1993 |
| Tune: | "Happy Birthday To You" |

| *Back Stamp* | *U.S. $* | *Price Can. $* | *U.K. £* | *Aust. $* |
|---|---|---|---|---|
| BK-4 | 75.00 | 100.00 | 55.00 | 100.00 |
| BK-5 | 75.00 | 100.00 | 55.00 | 100.00 |

**DB37**
**JOGGING BUNNYKINS™**
**Music Box**

| | |
|---|---|
| Designer: | Harry Sales |
| Modeller: | David Lyttleton |
| Height: | 5 1/2", 14.0 cm |
| Colour: | Yellow and blue |
| Issued: | 1987 - 1989 |
| Tune: | "King of the Road" |

| *Back Stamp* | *U.S. $* | *Price Can. $* | *U.K. £* | *Aust. $* |
|---|---|---|---|---|
| BK-5 | 125.00 | 150.00 | 75.00 | 125.00 |

**DB38**
**MR. BUNNYBEAT STRUMMING ™**
**Music Box**

| | |
|---|---|
| Designer: | Harry Sales |
| Modeller: | David Lyttleton |
| Height: | 7 1/2", 19.1 cm |
| Colour: | Pink, white and yellow |
| Issued: | 1987 - 1989 (©1987) |
| Tune: | "Hey Jude" |

| *Back Stamp* | *U.S. $* | *Price Can. $* | *U.K. £* | *Aust. $* |
|---|---|---|---|---|
| BK-5 | 225.00 | 150.00 | 75.00 | 125.00 |

**DB39**
**MRS. BUNNYKINS AT THE EASTER PARADE™**
**Music Box**

| | |
|---|---|
| Designer: | Harry Sales |
| Modeller: | David Lyttleton |
| Height: | 7", 17.8 cm |
| Colour: | Blue, yellow and maroon |
| Issued: | 1987 - 1991 (©1988) |
| Tune: | "Easter Parade" |

| *Back Stamp* | *U.S. $* | *Price Can. $* | *U.K. £* | *Aust. $* |
|---|---|---|---|---|
| BK-5 | 75.00 | 100.00 | 55.00 | 100.00 |

**DB40**
**AEROBIC BUNNYKINS™**

| | |
|---|---|
| Designer: | Harry Sales |
| Modeller: | David Lyttleton |
| Height: | 2 3/4", 7.0 cm |
| Colour: | Yellow and pale blue |
| Issued: | 1985 - 1988 (© 1984) |

"AEROBIC BUNNYKINS"
DB 40
© ROYAL DOULTON (UK) 1984

| *Back Stamp* | *U.S. $* | *Price Can. $* | *U.K. £* | *Aust. $* |
|---|---|---|---|---|
| BK-4 | 100.00 | 100.00 | 55.00 | 90.00 |
| BK-5 | 100.00 | 100.00 | 55.00 | 90.00 |

**DB41**
**FREEFALL BUNNYKINS™**

| | |
|---|---|
| Designer: | Harry Sales |
| Modeller: | David Lyttleton |
| Height: | 2 1/4", 5.7 cm |
| Colour: | Grey, yellow and white |
| Issued: | 1986 - 1989 (© 1984) |

"FREEFALL BUNNYKINS"
DB 41
© ROYAL DOULTON (UK) 1984

| *Back Stamp* | *U.S. $* | *Price Can. $* | *U.K. £* | *Aust. $* |
|---|---|---|---|---|
| BK-4 | 115.00 | 125.00 | 75.00 | 90.00 |
| BK-5 | 115.00 | 125.00 | 75.00 | 90.00 |

**DB42**
**ACE BUNNYKINS™**

| | |
|---|---|
| Designer: | Harry Sales |
| Modeller: | David Lyttleton |
| Height: | 3 3/4", 9.5 cm |
| Colour: | White and blue |
| Issued: | 1986 - 1989 (© 1985) |

ACE BUNNYKINS
DB 42
© ROYAL DOULTON (UK) 1985

| *Back Stamp* | *U.S. $* | *Price Can. $* | *U.K. £* | *Aust. $* |
|---|---|---|---|---|
| BK-4 | 100.00 | 100.00 | 55.00 | 90.00 |
| BK-5 | 100.00 | 100.00 | 55.00 | 90.00 |

**DB43**
**HOME RUN BUNNYKINS™**
**(1 on back of jersey)**

| | |
|---|---|
| Designer: | Harry Sales |
| Modeller: | David Lyttleton |
| Height: | 4", 10.1 cm |
| Colour: | Blue, yellow and white |
| Issued: | 1986 - 1993 (© 1985) |

HOME RUN BUNNYKINS
DB 43
© ROYAL DOULTON (UK) 1985

| *Back Stamp* | *U.S. $* | *Price Can. $* | *U.K. £* | *Aust. $* |
|---|---|---|---|---|
| BK-4 | 50.00 | 50.00 | 25.00 | 55.00 |
| BK-5 | 50.00 | 50.00 | 25.00 | 55.00 |

Note: The number DB 44 was assigned to the figurine "Ballet Bunnykins", however this figure was never issued.

**DB45**
**KING JOHN™**
**First Version**

| | |
|---|---|
| Designer: | Harry Sales |
| Modeller: | David Lyttleton |
| Height: | 4", 10.1 cm |
| Colour: | Red, yellow and blue |
| Issued: | 1986 - 1990 (© 1985) |
| Varieties: | DB91 |
| Series: | Bunnykins Royal Family |

BUNNYKINS ROYAL FAMILY
KING JOHN
DB 45
© 1985 ROYAL DOULTON (UK)

| *Back Stamp* | *U.S. $* | *Price Can. $* | *U.K. £* | *Aust. $* |
|---|---|---|---|---|
| BK-4 | 95.00 | 100.00 | 35.00 | 100.00 |
| BK-5 | 95.00 | 100.00 | 35.00 | 100.00 |
| Set DB45 - 49 5 pcs. | 400.00 | 450.00 | 175.00 | 375.00 |

**DB46**
**QUEEN SOPHIE™**
**First Version**

| | |
|---|---|
| Designer: | Harry Sales |
| Modeller: | David Lyttleton |
| Height: | 4 1/2", 11.4 cm |
| Colour: | Blue and red |
| Issued: | 1986 - 1990 (© 1985) |
| Varieties: | DB92 |
| Series: | Bunnykins Royal Family |

BUNNYKINS ROYAL FAMILY
QUEEN SOPHIE
DB46
© 1985 ROYAL DOULTON (U.K.)

| *Back Stamp* | *U.S. $* | *Price Can. $* | *U.K. £* | *Aust. $* |
|---|---|---|---|---|
| BK-4 | 95.00 | 100.00 | 35.00 | 75.00 |
| BK-5 | 95.00 | 100.00 | 35.00 | 75.00 |

**DB47**
**PRINCESS BEATRICE™**
**First Version**

| | |
|---|---|
| Designer: | Harry Sales |
| Modeller: | David Lyttleton |
| Height: | 3 1/2", 8.9 cm |
| Colour: | Pale green |
| Issued: | 1986 - 1990 (© 1985) |
| Varieties: | DB93 |
| Series: | Bunnykins Royal Family |

BUNNYKINS ROYAL FAMILY
PRINCESS BEATRICE

| *Back Stamp* | *U.S. $* | *Price Can. $* | *U.K. £* | *Aust. $* |
|---|---|---|---|---|
| BK-4 | 80.00 | 75.00 | 35.00 | 75.00 |
| BK-5 | 80.00 | 75.00 | 35.00 | 75.00 |

**DB48**
**PRINCE FREDERICK™**
**First Version**

| | |
|---|---|
| Designer: | Harry Sales |
| Modeller: | David Lyttleton |
| Height: | 3 1/2", 8.9 cm |
| Colour: | Green, white and red |
| Issued: | 1986 - 1990 |
| Varieties: | DB94 |
| Series: | Bunnykins Royal Family |

BUNNYKINS ROYAL FAMILY
PRINCE FREDERICK
DB 48
© 1985 ROYAL DOULTON (U.K.)

| *Back Stamp* | *U.S. $* | *Price Can. $* | *U.K. £* | *Aust. $* |
|---|---|---|---|---|
| BK-4 | 80.00 | 75.00 | 35.00 | 75.00 |
| BK-5 | 80.00 | 75.00 | 35.00 | 75.00 |

**DB49**
**HARRY THE HERALD™**
**First Version**

| | |
|---|---|
| Designer: | Harry Sales |
| Modeller: | David Lyttleton |
| Height: | 3 1/2", 8.9 cm |
| Colour: | Maroon, white and tan |
| Issued: | 1986 - 1990 (© 1985) |
| Varieties: | DB95, DB115 |
| Series: | Bunnykins Royal Family |

| *Back Stamp* | *U.S. $* | *Price Can. $* | *U.K. £* | *Aust. $* |
|---|---|---|---|---|
| BK-4 | 95.00 | 100.00 | 35.00 | 75.00 |
| BK-5 | 95.00 | 100.00 | 35.00 | 75.00 |

**DB50**
**UNCLE SAM BUNNYKINS™**

| | |
|---|---|
| Designer: | Harry Sales |
| Modeller: | David Lyttleton |
| Height: | 4 1/2", 11 cm |
| Colour: | Blue, red and white |
| Issued: | 1986 to the present (© 1985) |

**Note:** Made exclusively for the U.S. market

| *Back Stamp* | *U.S. $* | *Price Can. $* | *U.K. £* | *Aust. $* |
|---|---|---|---|---|
| BK-4 | 40.00 | 60.00 | 30.00 | 70.00 |
| BK-5 | 40.00 | 60.00 | 30.00 | 70.00 |

**DB51**
**MR. BUNNYKINS AT THE EASTER PARADE ™**
**Second Version**

| | |
|---|---|
| Designer: | Harry Sales |
| Modeller: | David Lyttleton |
| Height: | 5", 12.7 cm |
| Colour: | Blue tie and hat band, maroon coat, light grey trousers,pink ribbon on package |
| Issued: | 1986 - 1986 |
| Varieties: | DB18 |

**Note:** Made exclusively for distribution in the U.S. market at Beswick Artist Events

| *Back Stamp* | *U.S. $* | *Price Can. $* | *U.K. £* | *Aust. $* |
|---|---|---|---|---|
| BK-'Special' | 550.00 | 550.00 | 325.00 | 600.00 |

**DB52**
**MRS. BUNNYKINS AT THE EASTER PARADE™**
**Second Version**

| | |
|---|---|
| Designer: | Harry Sales |
| Modeller: | David Lyttleton |
| Height: | 4 1/2", 11.4 cm |
| Colour: | Maroon dress, white collar, blue bow on bonnet, multi-coloured bows on packages |
| Issued: | 1986 - 1986 |
| Varieties: | DB19 |

**Note:** Made exclusively for distribution in the U.S. market at Beswick Artist Events

| *Back Stamp* | *U.S. $* | *Price Can. $* | *U.K. £* | *Aust. $* |
|---|---|---|---|---|
| BK-'Special' | 650.00 | 750.00 | 375.00 | 750.00 |

**DB53**
**CAROL SINGER™**
**Music Box**

| | |
|---|---|
| Designer: | Harry Sales |
| Modeller: | David Lyttleton |
| Height: | 7", 17.8 cm |
| Colour: | Red, yellow and green |
| Issued: | 1986 - 1989 |
| Tune: | "Silent Night" |

| *Back Stamp* | *U.S. $* | *Price Can. $* | *U.K. £* | *Aust. $* |
|---|---|---|---|---|
| BK-4 | 125.00 | 150.00 | 75.00 | 125.00 |
| BK-5 | 125.00 | 150.00 | 75.00 | 125.00 |

**DB54**
**COLLECTOR BUNNYKINS™**

| | |
|---|---|
| Designer: | Harry Sales |
| Modeller: | David Lyttleton |
| Height: | 4 1/4", 10.8 cm |
| Colour: | Brown, blue and grey |
| Issued: | 1987 - 1987 |
| Series: | R.D.I.C.C. |

| *Back Stamp* | *U.S. $* | *Price Can. $* | *U.K. £* | *Aust. $* |
|---|---|---|---|---|
| BK-'Special' | 395.00 | 400.00 | 350.00 | 400.00 |

**DB55**
**BEDTIME BUNNYKINS™**
**First Version**

Designer: Graham Tongue
Modeller: David Lyttleton
Height: 3 1/4", 8.3 cm
Colour: Blue and white striped pyjamas, brown teddy bear
Issued: 1987 to the present (© 1986)
Varieties: DB63, 79, 103

| *Back Stamp* | *U.S. $* | *Price Can. $* | *U.K. £* | *Aust. $* |
|---|---|---|---|---|
| BK-5 | 40.00 | 52.00 | 13.50 | 65.00 |

**DB56**
**BE PREPARED BUNNYKINS™**

Designer: Graham Tongue
Modeller: David Lyttleton
Height: 4", 10.1 cm
Colour: Dark green and grey
Issued: 1987 to the present (© 1986)

| *Back Stamp* | *U.S. $* | *Price Can. $* | *U.K. £* | *Aust. $* |
|---|---|---|---|---|
| BK-5 | 40.00 | 52.00 | 13.50 | 57.00 |

**DB57**
**SCHOOL DAYS BUNNYKINS™**

Designer: Graham Tongue
Modeller: David Lyttleton
Height: 3 1/2", 8.9 cm
Colour: Dark green, white and yellow
Issued: 1987 to the present (© 1986)

| *Back Stamp* | *U.S. $* | *Price Can. $* | *U.K. £* | *Aust. $* |
|---|---|---|---|---|
| BK-5 | 40.00 | 52.00 | 13.50 | 57.00 |

**DB58**
**AUSTRALIAN BUNNYKINS™**

| | |
|---|---|
| Designer: | Harry Sales |
| Modeller: | Warren Platt |
| Height: | 4", 10.1 cm |
| Colour: | Gold and green |
| Issued: | 1988 - 1988 |

"AUSTRALIAN BUNNYKINS"
DB58
© 1987 ROYAL DOULTON

The
Australian Bicentenary
1788 - 1988 ©

**Note:** Sold exclusively in Australia celebrating the Australian Bicentenary

| *Back Stamp* | *U.S. $* | *Price Can. $* | *U.K. £* | *Aust. $* |
|---|---|---|---|---|
| BK-'Special' | 200.00 | 250.00 | 90.00 | 250.00 |

**DB59**
**STORYTIME BUNNYKINS™**
**Second Version**

| | |
|---|---|
| Designer: | Walter Hayward |
| Modeller: | Albert Hallam |
| Height: | 3", 7.6 cm |
| Colour: | Left: Green polka dots on white, yellow shoes<br>Right: Yellow dress, green shoes |
| Issued: | 1987 - 1987 (© 1974) |
| Varieties: | DB9 |

BUNNYKINS ®
"Storytime"
DB 59
© 1974 ROYAL DOULTON

**Note:** Produced for distribution at special events in the U.S.A.

| *Back Stamp* | *U.S. $* | *Price Can. $* | *U.K. £* | *Aust. $* |
|---|---|---|---|---|
| BK-'Special' | 125.00 | 150.00 | 90.00 | 90.00 |

**DB60**
**SCHOOLMASTER BUNNYKINS™**

| | |
|---|---|
| Designer: | Graham Tongue |
| Modeller: | Warren Platt |
| Height: | 4", 10 cm |
| Colour: | Black, white, green and white |
| Issued: | 1987 to the present (© 1987) |

SCHOOLMASTER BUNNYKINS
DB 60
© 1987 ROYAL DOULTON

| *Back Stamp* | *U.S. $* | *Price Can. $* | *U.K. £* | *Aust. $* |
|---|---|---|---|---|
| BK-5 | 40.00 | 52.00 | 14.95 | 57.00 |

**DB61**
**BROWNIE BUNNYKINS™**

| | |
|---|---|
| Designer: | Graham Tongue |
| Modeller: | Warren Platt |
| Height: | 4", 10 cm |
| Colour: | Brown uniform, yellow neck-tie |
| Issued: | 1987 - 1993 (© 1987) |

| *Back Stamp* | *U.S. $* | *Price Can. $* | *U.K. £* | *Aust. $* |
|---|---|---|---|---|
| BK-5 | 50.00 | 50.00 | 20.00 | 57.00 |

**DB62**
**SANTA BUNNYKINS HAPPY CHRISTMAS™**
**Christmas Tree Ornament**

| | |
|---|---|
| Designer: | Harry Sales |
| Modeller: | David Lyttleton |
| Height: | Unknown |
| Colour: | Red and white |
| Issued: | 1987 in a limited edition of 1551 |

| *Back Stamp* | *U.S. $* | *Price Can. $* | *U.K. £* | *Aust. $* |
|---|---|---|---|---|
| BK-"Special" | 1,300.00 | 900.00 | 450.00 | 800.00 |

**DB63**
**BEDTIME BUNNYKINS™**
**Second Version**

| | |
|---|---|
| Designer: | Graham Tongue |
| Modeller: | David Lyttleton |
| Height: | 3 1/4", 8.3 cm |
| Colour: | Red and white striped pyjamas, white teddy bear |
| Issued: | 1987 - 1987 (© 1986) |
| Varieties: | DB55, 79, 103 |

**Note:** Commissioned by D. H. Holmes, New Orleans, Louisianna

| *Back Stamp* | *U.S. $* | *Price Can. $* | *U.K. £* | *Aust. $* |
|---|---|---|---|---|
| BK-'Special' | 200.00 | 150.00 | 75.00 | 135.00 |

**DB64**
**POLICEMAN BUNNYKINS™**

| | |
|---|---|
| Designer: | Graham Tongue |
| Modeller: | Martyn Alcock |
| Height: | 4 1/4", 10.8 cm |
| Colour: | Dark blue uniform |
| Issued: | 1988 to the present (© 1987) |

| *Back Stamp* | *U.S. $* | *Price Can. $* | *U.K. £* | *Aust. $* |
|---|---|---|---|---|
| BK-5 | 40.00 | 44.00 | 13.50 | 57.00 |

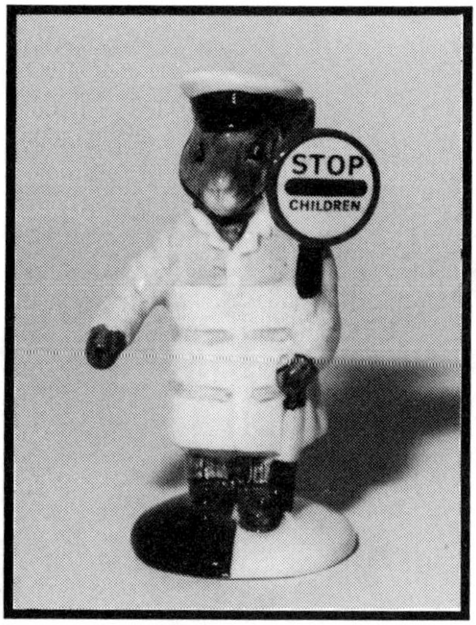


**DB65**
**LOLLIPOPMAN BUNNYKINS™**

| | |
|---|---|
| Designer: | Graham Tongue |
| Modeller: | Martyn Alcock |
| Height: | 3 3/4", 9.5 cm |
| Colour: | White and yellow |
| Issued: | 1988 - 1991 (Reg'd 1987) |

| *Back Stamp* | *U.S. $* | *Price Can. $* | *U.K. £* | *Aust. $* |
|---|---|---|---|---|
| BK-5 | 40.00 | 45.00 | 30.00 | 70.00 |

**DB66**
**SCHOOLBOY BUNNYKINS™**

| | |
|---|---|
| Designer: | Graham Tongue |
| Modeller: | Martyn Alcock |
| Height: | 4", 10.1 cm |
| Colour: | Blue, white and grey |
| Issued: | 1988 - 1991 (© 1987) |

| *Back Stamp* | *U.S. $* | *Price Can. $* | *U.K. £* | *Aust. $* |
|---|---|---|---|---|
| BK-5 | 40.00 | 45.00 | 13.00 | 57.00 |

**DB67**
**FAMILY PHOTOGRAPH™**
**Second Version**

| | |
|---|---|
| Designer: | Walter Hayward |
| Modeller: | Albert Hallam |
| Height: | 4 1/2", 11.4 cm |
| Colour: | Pink , black and white |
| Issued: | 1988 - 1988 (©1972) |
| Varieties: | DB1 |

BUNNYKINS ®
"Family Photograph"
DB67
© 1972 ROYAL DOULTON
NEW COLOURWAY 1988
SPECIAL EVENTS - USA 1988

**Note:** New colourway produced in 1988 for Special Events in the U.S.A. 1988

| *Back Stamp* | *U.S. $* | *Price Can. $* | *U.K. £* | *Aust. $* |
|---|---|---|---|---|
| BK-'Special' | 150.00 | 150.00 | 75.00 | 110.00 |

**DB68**
**FATHER, MOTHER AND VICTORIA BUNNYKINS™**

| | |
|---|---|
| Designer: | Based on design "Family Photograph" by Walter Hayward |
| Modeller: | Martyn Alcock |
| Height: | 4 1/2", 11.4 cm |
| Colour: | Blue, grey, maroon and yellow |
| Issued: | 1988 to the present (© 1988) |

FATHER, MOTHER
& VICTORIA BUNNYKINS
DB 68
© 1988 ROYAL DOULTON

| *Back Stamp* | *U.S. $* | *Price Can. $* | *U.K. £* | *Aust. $* |
|---|---|---|---|---|
| BK-5 | 40.00 | 52.00 | 14.95 | 67.00 |

**DB69**
**WILLIAM BUNNYKINS™**

| | |
|---|---|
| Designer: | Based on design by Walter Hayward |
| Modeller: | Martyn Alcock |
| Height: | Unknown |
| Colour: | Red and white |
| Issued: | 1988 - 1993 |

WILLIAM BUNNYKINS
DB 69
© 1988 ROYAL DOULTON

| *Back Stamp* | *U.S. $* | *Price Can. $* | *U.K. £* | *Aust. $* |
|---|---|---|---|---|
| BK-5 | 50.00 | 50.00 | 20.00 | 57.00 |

**DB70**
**SUSAN BUNNYKINS™**

Designer: Based on a design by Walter Hayward
Modeller: Martyn Alcock
Height: 3 1/4", 8.3 cm
Colour: White, blue and yellow
Issued: 1988 - 1993 (© 1988)

| *Back Stamp* | *U.S. $* | *Price Can. $* | *U.K. £* | *Aust. $* |
|---|---|---|---|---|
| BK-5 | 45.00 | 50.00 | 20.00 | 57.00 |

**DB71**
**POLLY BUNNYKINS™**

Designer: Graham Tongue
Modeller: Martyn Alcock
Height: 3 1/2", 8.7 cm
Colour: Pink
Issued: 1988 - 1993 (Reg'd 1988)

| *Back Stamp* | *U.S. $* | *Price Can. $* | *U.K. £* | *Aust. $* |
|---|---|---|---|---|
| BK-5 | 45.00 | 50.00 | 20.00 | 57.00 |

**DB72**
**TOM BUNNYKINS™**

Designer: Graham Tongue
Modeller: Martyn Alcock
Height: 3", 7.6 cm
Colour: Browns, white and blue
Issued: 1988 - 1993 (© 1988)

| *Back Stamp* | *U.S. $* | *Price Can. $* | *U.K. £* | *Aust. $* |
|---|---|---|---|---|
| BK-5 | 45.00 | 50.00 | 20.00 | 57.00 |

**DB73**
**HARRY BUNNYKINS™**

| | |
|---|---|
| Designer: | Graham Tongue |
| Modeller: | Martyn Alcock |
| Height: | 3", 7.9 cm |
| Colour: | Blue, brown, white and yellow |
| Issued: | 1988 - 1993 (© 1988) |

| *Back Stamp* | *U.S. $* | *Price Can. $* | *U.K. £* | *Aust. $* |
|---|---|---|---|---|
| BK-5 | 45.00 | 50.00 | 20.00 | 57.00 |

**DB74A**
**NURSE BUNNYKINS™**
**First Version - Red Cross**

| | |
|---|---|
| Designer: | Graham Tongue |
| Modeller: | Martyn Alcock |
| Height: | 4 1/4", 10.8 cm |
| Colour: | Dark and light blue and white, red cross. |
| Issued: | 1989 - 1994 (© 1988) |
| Varieties: | DB 74B |

| *Back Stamp* | *U.S. $* | *Price Can. $* | *U.K. £* | *Aust. $* |
|---|---|---|---|---|
| BK-5 | 100.00 | 100.00 | 50.00 | 100.00 |

**DB74B**
**NURSE BUNNYKINS™**
**Second Version - Green Cross**

| | |
|---|---|
| Designer: | Graham Tongue |
| Modeller: | Martyn Alcock |
| Height: | 4 1/4", 10.8 cm |
| Colour: | Dark and light blue and white, green cross. |
| Issued: | 1989 - 1994 (© 1988) |
| Varieties: | DB 74A |

| *Back Stamp* | *U.S. $* | *Price Can. $* | *U.K. £* | *Aust. $* |
|---|---|---|---|---|
| BK-5 | 35.00 | 45.00 | 13.50 | 55.00 |

**DB75**
**FIREMAN BUNNYKINS™**

Designer: Graham Tongue
Modeller: Martyn Alcock
Height: 4 1/4", 10.8 cm
Colour: Dark blue and yellow
Issued: 1989 to the present (© 1988)

FIREMAN BUNNYKINS
DB 75
© 1988 ROYAL DOULTON

| *Back Stamp* | *U.S. $* | *Price Can. $* | *U.K. £* | *Aust. $* |
|---|---|---|---|---|
| BK-5 | 40.00 | 52.00 | 14.95 | 57.00 |

**DB76**
**POSTMAN BUNNYKINS™**

Designer: Graham Tongue
Modeller: Martyn Alcock
Height: 4 1/2", 11.4 cm
Colour: Dark blue and red
Issued: 1989 - 1993 (© 1989)

POSTMAN BUNNYKINS
DB 76
© 1989 ROYAL DOULTON

| *Back Stamp* | *U.S. $* | *Price Can. $* | *U.K. £* | *Aust. $* |
|---|---|---|---|---|
| BK-5 | 50.00 | 50.00 | 25.00 | 57.00 |

**DB77**
**PAPERBOY BUNNYKINS ™**

Designer: Graham Tongue
Modeller: Martyn Alcock
Height: 4", 10.4 cm
Colour: Green, yellow, red and white
Issued: 1989 - 1993

PAPERBOY BUNNYKINS
DB 77
© 1989 ROYAL DOULTON

| *Back Stamp* | *U.S. $* | *Price Can. $* | *U.K. £* | *Aust. $* |
|---|---|---|---|---|
| BK-5 | 50.00 | 60.00 | 30.00 | 60.00 |

**DB78**
**TALLY HO! BUNNYKINS™**
**Second Version**

| | |
|---|---|
| Designer: | Based on a design by Walter Hayward |
| Modeller: | Albert Hallam |
| Height: | 4", 9.8 cm |
| Colour: | Light blue coat and white rocking horse, yellow sweater |
| Issued: | 1988 - 1988 (© 1974) |
| Varieties: | DB12 |

**Note:** Commissioned by Macy's Department Store, New York, N.Y.
Also painted in deeper shades of blue and yellow.

| *Back Stamp* | *U.S. $* | *Price Can. $* | *U.K. £* | *Aust. $* |
|---|---|---|---|---|
| BK-'Special' | 100.00 | 125.00 | 50.00 | 90.00 |

**DB79**
**BEDTIME BUNNYKINS™**
**Third Version**

| | |
|---|---|
| Designer: | Graham Tongue |
| Modeller: | David Lyttleton |
| Height: | 3 1/4", 8.3 cm |
| Colour: | Light blue and white |
| Issued: | 1988 - 1988 |
| Varieties: | DB55, 63, 103 |

**Note:** Belk Backstamp in a Special Commission Colourway of 100

| *Back Stamp* | *U.S. $* | *Price Can. $* | *U.K. £* | *Aust. $* |
|---|---|---|---|---|
| BK-'Special' | 850.00 | 1,000.00 | 600.00 | 1,000.00 |

**DB80**
**DOLLIE BUNNYKINS PLAYTIME ™**
**Seccond Version**

| | |
|---|---|
| Designer: | Based on a design by Walter Hayward |
| Modeller: | Albert Hallam |
| Height: | 4", 10.1 cm |
| Colour: | White and yellow |
| Issued: | 1988 - 1988 (© 1972) |
| Varieties: | DB8 |

**Note:** Issued for the "Doulton Rooms" in the U.S.A. 250 in each edition

| *Back Stamp* | *Type* | *U.S. $* | *Price Can. $* | *U.K. £* | *Aust. $* |
|---|---|---|---|---|---|
| BK-'Special' | "Higbee" | 125.00 | 150.00 | 55.00 | 165.00 |
| BK-'Special' | "Holmes " | 125.00 | 150.00 | 55.00 | 165.00 |
| BK-'Special' | "Hornes" | 125.00 | 150.00 | 55.00 | 165.00 |
| BK-'Special' | "Strawbridge" | 125.00 | 150.00 | 55.00 | 165.00 |

**DB81**
**BILLIE & BUNTIE BUNNYKINS SLEIGH RIDE™**
**Second Version**

| | |
|---|---|
| Designer: | Based on a design by Walter Hayward |
| Modeller: | Albert Hallam |
| Height: | 3 1/2", 8.9 cm |
| Colour: | Green, yellow and red |
| Issued: | 1989 - 1989 (© 1972) |
| Varieties: | DB4 |

**Note:** Special Events Tour 1989

| *Back Stamp* | *U.S. $* | *Price Can. $* | *U.K. £* | *Aust. $* |
|---|---|---|---|---|
| Backstamp 'Special' | 100.00 | 100.00 | 75.00 | 90.00 |

**DB82**
**ICE CREAM BUNNYKINS™**

| | |
|---|---|
| Designer: | Graham Tongue |
| Modeller: | Warren Platt |
| Height: | 4 1/2", 11.4 cm |
| Colour: | White, blue and green |
| Issued: | 1990 - 1993 (©1989) |

ICE CREAM BUNNYKINS
DB 82
© 1989 ROYAL DOULTON

| *Back Stamp* | *U.S. $* | *Price Can. $* | *U.K. £* | *Aust. $* |
|---|---|---|---|---|
| BK-5 | 65.00 | 75.00 | 35.00 | 65.00 |

**DB83**
**SUSAN BUNNYKINS AS QUEEN OF THE MAY™**

| | |
|---|---|
| Designer: | Graham Tongue |
| Modeller: | Martyn Alcock |
| Height: | 4", 10.2 cm |
| Colour: | White polka dot dress, blue and brown chair |
| Issued: | 1990 - 1991 © 1989 |

SUSAN BUNNYKINS
AS QUEEN OF THE MAY
DB 83
© 1989 ROYAL DOULTON

| *Back Stamp* | *U.S. $* | *Price Can. $* | *U.K. £* | *Aust. $* |
|---|---|---|---|---|
| BK-5 | 50.00 | 65.00 | 35.00 | 67.00 |

### DB84
### FISHERMAN BUNNYKINS™

| | |
|---|---|
| Designer: | Graham Tongue |
| Modeller: | Warren Platt |
| Height: | 4 1/4", 10.8 cm |
| Colour: | Maroon, yellow and grey |
| Issued: | 1990 - 1993 (© 1990) |

| *Back Stamp* | *U.S. $* | *Price Can. $* | *U.K. £* | *Aust. $* |
|---|---|---|---|---|
| BK-5 | 75.00 | 80.00 | 40.00 | 80.00 |

### DB85
### COOK BUNNYKINS™

| | |
|---|---|
| Designer: | Graham Tongue |
| Modeller: | Warren Platt |
| Height: | 4 1/4", 10.8 cm |
| Colour: | White and green |
| Issued: | 1990 to the present (© 1990) |

| *Back Stamp* | *U.S. $* | *Price Can. $* | *U.K. £* | *Aust. $* |
|---|---|---|---|---|
| BK-5 | 35.00 | 44.00 | 13.50 | 55.00 |

### DB86
### SOUSAPHONE BUNNYKINS™
**From the Oompah Band - Second Version**

| | |
|---|---|
| Designer: | Harry Sales |
| Modeller: | David Lyttleton |
| Height: | 3 1/2", 8.9 cm |
| Colour: | Blue uniform and yellow sousaphone |
| Issued: | 1990 in a limited edition of 250 sets (© 1990) |
| Series: | Royal Doulton Collectors Band |
| Varieties: | DB23, 105 |

**Note:** Special colourway edition of 250 Exclusive for U.K. Fairs Ltd.

| *Back Stamp* | *U.S. $* | *Price Can. $* | *U.K. £* | *Aust. $* |
|---|---|---|---|---|
| BK-"U.K. Fairs" DB86 to 90 5 pcs. | 150.00 | 200.00 | 100.00 | 110.00 |

IPETER BUNNYKINS
I THE OOMPAH BAND
DB 87
1990 ROYAL DOULTON

.K. Fairs Ltd.

| | Price | | |
|---|---|---|---|
| . $ | U.K. £ | Aust. $ |
| 00 | 100.00 | 110.00 |

UNNYKINS™
mpah Band - Second Version

Harry Sales
David Lyttleton
3 1/2", 8.9 cm
Blue uniform and yellow cymbals
1990 in a limited edition of 250 sets
Royal Doulton Collectors Band
DB25, 107

"CYMBAL BUNNYKINS"
FROM THE OOMPAH BAND
DB 88
© 1990 ROYAL DOULTON

l colourway edition of 250 Exclusive for U.K. Fairs Ltd.

| | | Price | | |
|---|---|---|---|---|
| | U.S. $ | Can. $ | U.K. £ | Aust. $ |
| l' | 125.00 | 200.00 | 100.00 | 110.00 |

**DRUMMER BUNNYKINS**
**Third Version**

Designer: Harry Sales
Modeller: David Lyttleton
Height: 3 3/4", 9.5 cm
Colour: Blue trousers and sleeves, yellow vest, cream and red drum
Issued: 1990 in a limited edition of 250 sets (© 1990)
Series: Royal Doulton Collectors Band
Varieties: DB26, 26A, 26B, 108

"DRUMMER BUNNYKINS"
FROM THE OOMPAH BAND
DB 89
SPECIAL COLOURWAY EDITION OF 250 SETS
EXCLUSIVE FOR UK FAIRS LTD.
© 1990 ROYAL DOULTON

**Note:** Special colourway edition of 250 Exclusive for U.K. Fairs Ltd.

| Back Stamp | U.S. $ | Price Can. $ | U.K. £ | Aust. $ |
|---|---|---|---|---|
| BK-'Special' | 195.00 | 200.00 | 100.00 | 150.00 |

## DB90
## DRUM-MAJOR BUNNYKINS™
**Second Version**

Designer: Harry Sales
Modeller: David Lyttleton
Height: 3 3/4", 9.5 cm
Colour: Blue and yellow uniform
Issued: 1990 in a limited edition of 250 sets
Series: Royal Doulton Collectors Band
Varieties: DB27, 109

DRUM-MAJOR BUNNYKINS
FROM THE OOMPAH BAND
DB 90
© 1990 ROYAL DOULTON

**Note:** Special colourway edition of 250 Exclusive for U.K. Fairs Ltd.

| *Back Stamp* | *U.S. $* | *Price Can. $* | *U.K. £* | *Aust. $* |
|---|---|---|---|---|
| BK-'Special' | 125.00 | 150.00 | 100.00 | 150.00 |

## DB91
## KING JOHN™
**Second Version**

BUNNYKINS ROYAL FAMILY
KING JOHN
DB 91
EXCLUSIVE COLOURWAY OF 250 SETS
FOR UK I CERAMICS LTD
© 1990 ROYAL DOULTON

Designer: Harry Sales
Modeller: David Lyttleton
Height: 4", 10.1 cm
Colour: Purple, yellow and white
Issued: 1990 in a limited edition of 250 sets (© 1990)
Series: Bunnykins Royal Family
Varieties: DB45

**Note:** Exclusive colourway of 250 sets for U.K. International Ceramics Ltd.

| *Back Stamp* | *U.S. $* | *Price Can. $* | *U.K. £* | *Aust. $* |
|---|---|---|---|---|
| BK-'Special' | 100.00 | 100.00 | 40.00 | 100.00 |
| Set DB91 - 95 (5 Pcs) | 400.00 | 500.00 | 250.00 | 500.00 |

## DB92
## QUEEN SOPHIE™
**Second Version**

Designer: Harry Sales
Modeller: David Lyttleton
Height: 4 1/2", 11.4 cm
Colour: Pink and purple
Issued: 1990 in a limited edition of 250 (© 1990)
Series: Bunnykins Royal Family
Varieties: DB46

BUNNYKINS ROYAL FAMILY
QUEEN SOPHIE
DB 92
© 1990 ROYAL DOULTON

**Note:** Exclusive colourway of 250 sets. For U.K. International Ceramics Ltd.

| *Back Stamp* | *U.S. $* | *Price Can. $* | *U.K. £* | *Aust. $* |
|---|---|---|---|---|
| BK-'Special' | 100.00 | 100.00 | 40.00 | 100.00 |

**DB93**
**PRINCESS BEATRICE™**
**Second Version**

| | |
|---|---|
| Designer: | Harry Sales |
| Modeller: | David Lyttleton |
| Height: | 3 1/2", 8.9 cm |
| Colour: | Yellow and gold |
| Issued: | 1990 in a limited edition of 250 (© 1990) |
| Series: | Bunnykins Royal Family |
| Varieties: | DB47 |

**Note:** Exclusive colourway of 250 sets. For U.K. International Ceramics Ltd.

| *Back Stamp* | *U.S. $* | *Price Can. $* | *U.K. £* | *Aust. $* |
|---|---|---|---|---|
| BK-'Special' | 90.00 | 100.00 | 40.00 | 100.00 |

**DB94**
**PRINCE FREDERICK™**
**Second Version**

| | |
|---|---|
| Designer: | Harry Sales |
| Modeller: | David Lyttleton |
| Height: | 3 1/2", 8.9 cm |
| Colour: | Red, blue and yellow |
| Issued: | 1990 in a limited edition of 250 (© 1990) |
| Series: | Bunnykins Royal Family |
| Varieties: | DB48 |

**Note:** Exclusive colourway of 250 sets. For U.K. International Ceramics Ltd.

| *Back Stamp* | *U.S. $* | *Price Can. $* | *U.K. £* | *Aust. $* |
|---|---|---|---|---|
| BK-'Special' | 90.00 | 100.00 | 40.00 | 100.00 |

**DB95**
**HARRY THE HERALD™**
**Second Version**

| | |
|---|---|
| Designer: | Harry Sales |
| Modeller: | David Lyttleton |
| Height: | 3 1/2", 8.9 cm |
| Colour: | Blue, red and yellow |
| Issued: | 1990 in a limited edition of 250 (© 1990) |
| Series: | Bunnykins Royal Family |
| Varieties: | DB49, 115 |

Note: Exclusive colourway of 250 sets. For U.K. International Ceramics Ltd.

| *Back Stamp* | *U.S. $* | *Price Can. $* | *U.K. £* | *Aust. $* |
|---|---|---|---|---|
| BK-'Special' | 100.00 | 125.00 | 75.00 | 125.00 |

**DB96**
**TOUCHDOWN BUNNYKINS™**
**Ohio State University - Third Version**

Designer: Harry Sales
Modeller: David Lyttleton
Height: 3 1/4", 8.3 cm
Colour: Grey and orange
Issued: 1990 in a limited edition of 200
Varieties: DB29, 29A, 29B, 97, 98, 99, 100

MADE IN ENGLAND ROYAL DOULTON ENGLAND
"TOUCHDOWN BUNNYKINS"
DB96
© 1990 ROYAL DOULTON

**Note:** Issued in a Limited Edition of 200

| *Back Stamp* | *U.S. $* | *Price Can. $* | *U.K. £* | *Aust. $* |
|---|---|---|---|---|
| BK-'Special' | 90.00 | 100.00 | 50.00 | 100.00 |
| Set, DB96-100 (5 pcs) | 400.00 | 500.00 | 225.00 | 500.00 |

**DB97**
**TOUCHDOWN BUNNYKINS™**
**University of Michigan - Fourth Version**

Designer: Harry Sales
Modeller: David Lyttleton
Height: 3 1/4", 8.3 cm
Colour: Yellow and blue
Issued: 1990 in a limited edition of 200
Varieties: DB29, 96, 98, 99, 100

MADE IN ENGLAND ROYAL DOULTON ENGLAND
"TOUCHDOWN BUNNYKINS"
DB97
© 1990 ROYAL DOULTON

**Note:** Issed in a Limited Edition of 200

| *Back Stamp* | *U.S. $* | *Price Can. $* | *U.K. £* | *Aust. $* |
|---|---|---|---|---|
| BK-'Special' | 90.00 | 100.00 | 50.00 | 100.00 |

**DB98**
**TOUCHDOWN BUNNYKINS™**
**Cincinnati Bengals - Fifth Version**

Designer: Harry Sales
Modeller: David Lyttleton
Height: 3 1/2", 8.3 cm
Colour: Orange and black
Issued: 1990 (©1990)
Varieties: DB29, 96, 97, 99, 100

MADE IN ENGLAND ROYAL DOULTON ENGLAND
"TOUCHDOWN BUNNYKINS"
DB98
© 1990 ROYAL DOULTON

**Note:** Issued in a Limited Edition of 200

| *Back Stamp* | *U.S. $* | *Price Can. $* | *U.K. £* | *Aust. $* |
|---|---|---|---|---|
| BK-'Special' | 90.00 | 100.00 | 50.00 | 100.00 |

**DB99**
**TOUCHDOWN BUNNYKINS™**
**Notre Dame College - Sixth Version**

| | |
|---|---|
| Designer: | Harry Sales |
| Modeller: | David Lyttleton |
| Height: | 3 1/2", 8.3 cm |
| Colour: | Green and yellow |
| Issued: | 1990 (©1990) |
| Varieties: | DB29, 96, 97, 98, 100 |

"TOUCHDOWN BUNNYKINS"
DB99
© 1990 ROYAL DOULTON

Note: Issued in a Limited Edition of 200

| *Back Stamp* | *U.S. $* | *Price Can. $* | *U.K. £* | *Aust. $* |
|---|---|---|---|---|
| BK-'Special' | 90.00 | 100.00 | 50.00 | 100.00 |

**DB100**
**TOUCHDOWN BUNNYKINS™**
**University of Indiana - Seventh Version**

| | |
|---|---|
| Designer: | Harry Sales |
| Modeller: | David Lyttleton |
| Height: | 3 1/2", 8.3 cm |
| Colour: | White and red |
| Issued: | 1990 (©1990) |
| Varieties: | DB29, 96, 97, 98, 99 |

"TOUCHDOWN BUNNYKINS"
DB100
© 1990 ROYAL DOULTON

**Note:** Issued in a Limited Edition of 200

| *Back Stamp* | *U.S. $* | *Price Can. $* | *U.K. £* | *Aust. $* |
|---|---|---|---|---|
| BK-'Special' | 90.00 | 100.00 | 50.00 | 100.00 |

**DB101**
**BRIDE BUNNYKINS™**

| | |
|---|---|
| Designer: | Graham Tongue |
| Modeller: | Amanda Hughes-Lubeck |
| Height: | 4", 10.1 cm |
| Colour: | Cream dress, grey, blue and white train |
| Issued: | 1991 to the present (©1990) |

BRIDE BUNNYKINS
DB101
© 1990 ROYAL DOULTON

| *Back Stamp* | *U.S. $* | *Price Can. $* | *U.K. £* | *Aust. $* |
|---|---|---|---|---|
| BK-5 | 40.00 | 59.50 | 16.95 | 67.00 |

**DB102**
**GROOM BUNNYKINS™**

| | |
|---|---|
| Designer: | Graham Tonge |
| Modeller: | Martyn Alcock |
| Height: | 4 1/2", 11.4 cm |
| Colour: | Grey and burgundy |
| Issued: | 1991 to the present (©1990) |

GROOM BUNNYKINS
DB 102
© 1990 ROYAL DOULTON

| *Back Stamp* | *U.S. $* | *Price Can. $* | *U.K. £* | *Aust. 4* |
|---|---|---|---|---|
| BK-5 | 40.00 | 59.50 | 16.95 | 67.00 |

**DB103**
**BEDTIME BUNNYKINS™**
**Fourth Version**

| | |
|---|---|
| Designer: | Graham Tongue |
| Modeller: | David Lyttleton |
| Height: | 3 1/4", 8.3 cm |
| Colour: | Yellow and green striped pyjamas, brown teddy bear |
| Issued: | 1991 - 1991 (©1986) |
| Varieties: | DB55, 63, 79 |

BEDTIME BUNNYKINS
DB 103
© 1986 ROYAL DOULTON
U.S. SPECIAL EVENTS TOUR 1991

**Note:** U.S. Special Events Tour 1991

| *Back Stamp* | *Type* | *U.S. $* | *Price Can. $* | *U.K. £* | *Aust. $* |
|---|---|---|---|---|---|
| BK-'Special' | Pale Yellow | 100.00 | 100.00 | 75.00 | 85.00 |
| BK-'Special' | Daffodil Yellow | 100.00 | 100.00 | 75.00 | 85.00 |

**DB104**
**CAROL SINGER BUNNYKINS™**

| | |
|---|---|
| Designer: | Harry Sales |
| Modeller: | David Lyttleton |
| Height: | 4", 10.1 cm |
| Colour: | Dark green, red, yellow and white |
| Issued: | 1991 (© 1986) |

SPECIAL EDITION OF 1000 EXCLUSIVE FOR U.K. INTERNATIONAL CERAMICS
CAROL SINGER BUNNYKINS
DB 104
© 1986 ROYAL DOULTON

**Note:** Special edition of 1000. Exclusive U.K. International Ceramics Ltd. 300 of edition have U.S.A. on backstamp

| *Back Stamp* | *U.S. $* | *Price Can. $* | *U.K.£* | *Aust. $* |
|---|---|---|---|---|
| BK-'Special' | 100.00 | 100.00 | 45.00 | 110.00 |

**DB105**
**SOUSAPHONE BUNNYKINS™**
**From the Oompah Band - Third Version**

| | |
|---|---|
| Designer: | Harry Sales |
| Modeller: | David Lyttleton |
| Height: | 4", 10.1 cm |
| Colour: | Dark green, red and yellow |
| Issued: | 1991 (© 1991) |
| Series: | Royal Doulton Collectors Band |
| Varieties: | DB 23, 86 |

**Note:** Issued in a Special Edition of 250 exclusive to U.K. Int'l Ceramics Ltd.

| *Back Stamp* | *Price U.S. $* | *Can. $* | *U.K. £* | *Aust. $* |
|---|---|---|---|---|
| BK-'Special' | 150.00 | 110.00 | 50.00 | 110.00 |
| Set DB 105 to 109 5 pcs. | | | 250.00 | |

**DB106**
**TRUMPETER BUNNYKINS™**
**From the Oompah Band - Third Version**

| | |
|---|---|
| Designer: | Harry Sales |
| Modeller: | David Lyttleton |
| Height: | 3 3/4", 9.5 cm |
| Colour: | Dark green, red and yellow |
| Issued: | 1991 (© 1991) |
| Series: | Royal Doulton Collectors Band |
| Varieties: | DB 24, 87 |

**Note:** Issued in a Special Edition of 250 exclusive to U.K. Int'l Ceramics Ltd.

| *Back Stamp* | *Price U.S. $* | *Can. $* | *U.K. £* | *Aust. $* |
|---|---|---|---|---|
| BK-'Special' | 125.00 | 110.00 | 50.00 | 110.00 |

**DB107**
**CYMBALS BUNNYKINS™**
**From the Oompah Band - Third Version**

| | |
|---|---|
| Designer: | Harry Sales |
| Modeller: | David Lyttleton |
| Height: | 4", 10.1 cm |
| Colour: | Dark green, red and yellow |
| Issued: | 1991 (© 1991) |
| Series: | Royal Doulton Collectors Band |
| Varieties: | DB 25, 88 |

**Note:** Issued in a Special Edition of 250 exclusive to U.K. Int'l Ceramics Ltd.

| *Back Stamp* | *Price U.S. $* | *Can. $* | *U.K. £* | *Aust. $* |
|---|---|---|---|---|
| BK-'Special' | 125.00 | 110.00 | 50.00 | 110.00 |

**DB 108**
**DRUMMER BUNNYKINS™**
**Fourth Version**

| | |
|---|---|
| Designer: | Harry Sales |
| Modeller: | David Lyttleton |
| Height: | 3 1/2", 8.9 cm |
| Colour: | Dark green, red and white |
| Issued: | 1991 (@ 1991) |
| Series: | Royal Doulton Collectors Band |
| Varieties: | DB 26, 26A, 26B, 89 |

"DRUMMER BUNNYKINS"
FROM THE OOMPAH BAND
DB 108
SPECIAL COLOURWAY EDITION OF 250 SETS
EXCLUSIVE FOR UK.FAIRS LTD.
© 1991 ROYAL DOULTON

**Note:** Special colourway edition of 250. Exclusive to U.K. Fairs Ltd.

| *Back Stamp* | *U.S. $* | *Price Can. $* | *U.K. £* | *Aust. $* |
|---|---|---|---|---|
| BK-'Special' | 195.00 | 110.00 | 50.00 | 150.00 |

**DB 109**
**DRUM-MAJOR BUNNYKINS™**
**From the Oompah Band - Third Version**

| | |
|---|---|
| Designer: | Harry Sales |
| Modeller: | David Lyttleton |
| Height: | 3 1/2", 8.9 cm |
| Colour: | Dark green, red and yellow |
| Issued: | 1991 (© 1991) |
| Series: | Royal Doulton Collectors Band |
| Varieties: | DB 27, 90 |

DRUM-MAJOR BUNNYKINS
FROM THE OOMPAH BAND
DB 109
© 1991 ROYAL DOULTON

**Note:** Special colourway edition of 250. Exclusive to U.K. Int'l Ceramics Ltd

| *Back Stamp* | *U.S. $* | *Price Can. $* | *U.K. £* | *Aust. $* |
|---|---|---|---|---|
| BK-'Special' | 125.00 | 110.00 | 50.00 | 120.00 |

Note: DB 110 to 114 not issued

**DB115**
**HARRY THE HERALD™**
**Third Version**

| | |
|---|---|
| Designer: | Harry Sales |
| Modeller: | David Lyttleton |
| Height: | 3 1/2", 8.9 cm |
| Colour: | Yellow and dark blue |
| Issued: | 1991 |
| Series: | Bunnykins Royal Family |
| Varieties: | DB 49, 95 |

**Note: Commissioned by Lambeth Productions in a special edition of 300.**

| *Back Stamp* | *U.S. $* | *Price Can. $* | *U.K. £* | *Aust. $* |
|---|---|---|---|---|
| BK-'Special' | 250.00 | 300.00 | 150.00 | 250.00 |

**DB116**
**GOALKEEPER BUNNYKINS ™**
**First Version**

| | |
|---|---|
| Designer: | Denise Andrews |
| Modeller: | Warren Platt |
| Height: | 4 1/2", 11.4 cm |
| Colour: | Green and black |
| Issued: | 1991 (© 1991) |
| Series: | Footballers |
| Varieties: | DB 118, 120, 122 |

GOALKEEPER BUNNYKINS
DB 116
© 1991 ROYAL DOULTON
EXCLUSIVELY PRODUCED FOR
U.K. INTERNATIONAL CERAMICS LTD.
SPECIAL EDITION OF 250 SETS

Note: Exclusive to U.K. International Ceramics Ltd. Special edition of 250

| *Back Stamp* | *U.S. $* | *Price Can. $* | *U.K. £* | *Aust. $* |
|---|---|---|---|---|
| BK-'Special' | 75.00 | 100.00 | 50.00 | 125.00 |

**DB117**
**FOOTBALLER BUNNYKINS™**
**First Version**

| | |
|---|---|
| Designer: | Denise Andrews |
| Modeller: | Warren Platt |
| Height: | 4 1/2", 11.4 cm |
| Colour: | Green and white |
| Issued: | 1991 (© 1991) |
| Series: | Footballers |
| Varieties: | DB 119, 121; Also called "Soccer Player" DB123 |

FOOTBALLER BUNNYKINS
DB 117
© 1991 ROYAL DOULTON
EXCLUSIVELY PRODUCED FOR
U.K. INTERNATIONAL CERAMICS LTD.
SPECIAL EDITION OF 250 SETS

**Note:** Exclusive to U.K. International Ceramics Ltd. Special edition of 250

| *Back Stamp* | *U.S. $* | *Price Can. $* | *U.K. £* | *Aust. $* |
|---|---|---|---|---|
| BK-'Special' | 85.00 | 100.00 | 50.00 | 125.00 |

**DB118**
**GOALKEEPER BUNNYKINS ™**
**Second Version**

| | |
|---|---|
| Designer: | Denise Andrews |
| Modeller: | Warren Platt |
| Height: | 4 1/2", 11.4 cm |
| Colour: | Red and black |
| Issued: | 1991 (© 1991) |
| Series: | Footballers |
| Varieties: | DB 116, 120, 122 |

GOALKEEPER BUNNYKINS
DB 118
© 1991 ROYAL DOULTON
EXCLUSIVELY PRODUCED FOR
U.K. INTERNATIONAL CERAMICS LTD
SPECIAL EDITION OF 250 SETS

**Note:** Exclusive to U.K. International Ceramics Ltd. Special edition of 250

| *Back Stamp* | *U.S. $* | *Price Can. $* | *U.K. £* | *Aust. $* |
|---|---|---|---|---|
| BK-'Special' | 75.00 | 100.00 | 40.00 | 125.00 |

## DB119
## FOOTBALLER BUNNYKINS ™
### Second Version

| | |
|---|---|
| Designer: | Denise Andrews |
| Modeller: | Warren Platt |
| Height: | 4 1/2", 11.4 cm |
| Colour: | Red |
| Issued: | 1991 (© 1991) |
| Series: | Footballers |
| Varieties: | DB 117, 121; Also called "Soccer Player" DB123 |

FOOTBALLER BUNNYKINS
DB 119
© 1991 ROYAL DOULTON
EXCLUSIVELY PRODUCED FOR
U.K. INTERNATIONAL CERAMICS LTD
SPECIAL EDITION OF 250 SETS

**Note:** Exclusive to U.K. International Ceramics Ltd. Special edition of 250

| *Back Stamp* | *U.S. $* | *Price Can. $* | *U.K. £* | *Aust. $* |
|---|---|---|---|---|
| BK-'Special' | 75.00 | 100.00 | 40.00 | 125.00 |

## DB120
## GOALKEEPER BUNNYKINS ™
### Third Version

| | |
|---|---|
| Designer: | Denise Andrews |
| Modeller: | Warren Platt |
| Height: | 4 1/2", 11.4 cm |
| Colour: | Yellow and black |
| Issued: | 1991 (© 1991) |
| Series: | Footballers |
| Varieties: | DB 116, 118, 122 |

GOALKEEPER BUNNYKINS
DB 120
© 1991 ROYAL DOULTON
EXCLUSIVELY PRODUCED FOR
U.K. INTERNATIONAL CERAMICS LTD
SPECIAL DOULTON FAIR EDITION
OF 250 SETS

**Note:** Exclusive to U.K. International Ceramics Ltd. Special edition of 250

| *Back Stamp* | *U.S. $* | *Price Can. $* | *U.K. £* | *Aust. $* |
|---|---|---|---|---|
| BK-'Special' | 75.00 | 100.00 | 50.00 | 120.00 |

## DB121
## FOOTBALLER BUNNYKINS ™
### Third Version

| | |
|---|---|
| Designer: | Denise Andrews |
| Modeller: | Warren Platt |
| Height: | 4 1/2", 11.4 cm |
| Colour: | White and blue |
| Issued: | 1991 (© 1991) |
| Series: | Footballers |
| Varieties: | DB 117, 119; Also called "Soccer Player" DB123 |

FOOTBALLER BUNNYKINS
DB 121
© 1991 ROYAL DOULTON
EXCLUSIVELY PRODUCED FOR
U.K. INTERNATIONAL CERAMICS LTD
SPECIAL DOULTON FAIR EDITION
OF 250 SETS

Note: Exclusive to U.K. International Ceramics Ltd. Special edition of 250 sets

| *Back Stamp* | *U.S. $* | *Price Can. $* | *U.K. £* | *Aust. $* |
|---|---|---|---|---|
| BK-'Special' | 75.00 | 100.00 | 50.00 | 125.00 |

## DB122
## GOALKEEPER BUNNYKINS ™
### Fourth Version

| | |
|---|---|
| Designer: | Denise Andrews |
| Modeller: | Warren Platt |
| Height: | 4 1/2", 1.4 cm |
| Colour: | Grey and black |
| Issued: | 1991 (©1991) |
| Series: | Footballers |
| Varieties: | DB 118, 118, 120 |

GOALKEEPER BUNNYKINS
DB 122
© 1991 ROYAL DOULTON
EXCLUSIVELY PRODUCED FOR
U.K. INTERNATIONAL CERAMICS LTD
SPECIAL EDITION OF 250 SETS

**Note:** Exclusive to U.K. International Ceramics Ltd. Special edition of 250

| *Back Stamp* | *U.S. $* | *Price Can. $* | *U.K. £* | *Aust. $* |
|---|---|---|---|---|
| BK-'Special' | 75.00 | 100.00 | 50.00 | 125.00 |

## DB123
## SOCCER PLAYER BUNNYKINS ™
### Fourth Version

| | |
|---|---|
| Designer: | Denise Andrews |
| Modeller: | Warren Platt |
| Height: | 4 1/2", 11.4 cm |
| Colour: | Dark blue and white |
| Issued: | 1991 (© 1991) |
| Series: | Footballers |
| Varieties: | DB 117, 119, 121 |

SOCCER PLAYER BUNNYKINS
DB 123
© 1991 ROYAL DOULTON
EXCLUSIVELY PRODUCED FOR
U.K. INTERNATIONAL CERAMICS LTD
SPECIAL EDITION OF 250 SETS

Note: Exclusive to U.K. International Ceramics Ltd. Special edition of 250 sets

| *Bacl Stamp* | *U.S. $* | *Price Can. $* | *U.K. £* | *Aust. $* |
|---|---|---|---|---|
| BK-'Special' | 75.00 | 100.00 | 50.00 | 125.00 |

## DB124
## ROCK 'N' ROLL BUNNYKINS™

| | |
|---|---|
| Designer: | Harry Sales |
| Modeller: | David Lyttleton |
| Height: | 4 1/2", 11.4 cm |
| Colour: | White, blue and red |
| Issued: | 1991 (© 1991) |

ROCK AND ROLL BUNNYKINS
DB 124
PRODUCED EXCLUSIVELY
FOR ROYAL DOULTON USA
ROCK AND ROLL HALL OF FAME EDITION
LIMITED TO 1000
THIS IS No 251
© 1991 ROYAL DOULTON

**Note:** Produced exclusively for Royal Doulton U.S.A. and Rock and Roll Hall of Fame, Cleveland. Limited Edition of 1000

| *Back Stamp* | *U.S. $* | *Price Can. $* | *U.K. £* | *Aust. $* |
|---|---|---|---|---|
| BK-'Special' | 125.00 | 150.00 | 75.00 | 165.00 |

**DB125**
**MILKMAN BUNNYKINS™**

| | |
|---|---|
| Designer: | Graham Tongue |
| Modeller: | Amanda Hughes-Lubeck |
| Height: | 4 1/2", 11.4 cm |
| Colour: | White, green and grey |
| Issued: | 1992 (© 1991) |

MILKMAN BUNNYKINS
DB 125
© 1991 ROYAL DOULTON
EXCLUSIVELY PRODUCED FOR
U.K. INTERNATIONAL CERAMICS LTD
SPECIAL EDITION OF 1,000 PIECES

**Note:** Commissioned by U.K. International Ceramics Ltd. in a special edition of 1,000.

| *Back Stamp* | *U.S. $* | *Price Can. $* | *U.K. £* | *Aust. $* |
|---|---|---|---|---|
| BK-'Special' | 95.00 | 100.00 | 45.00 | 100.00 |

**DB126**
**MAGICIAN BUNNYKINS™**

| | |
|---|---|
| Designer: | Graham Tongue |
| Modeller: | Warren Platt |
| Height: | 4 1/2", 11.4 cm |
| Colour: | Black and yellow |
| Issued: | 1992 (© 1992) |

MAGICIAN BUNNYKINS
DB 126
© 1992 ROYAL DOULTON

**Note:** Commissioned by Pascoe & Co. and Charles Dombeck

| *Back Stamp* | *U.S. $* | *Price Can. $* | *U.K. £* | *Aust. $* |
|---|---|---|---|---|
| BK-'Special' | 75.00 | 100.00 | 55.00 | 100.00 |

**DB127**
**GUARDSMAN BUNNYKINS™**

| | |
|---|---|
| Designer: | Denise Andrews |
| Modeller: | Warren Platt |
| Height: | 4 1/2", 11.4 cm |
| Colour: | Scarlet jacket, black trousers and bearskin hat |
| Issued: | 1992 (© 1992) |

GUARDSMAN BUNNYKINS
DB 127
PRODUCED EXCLUSIVELY
FOR U.K.I. CERAMICS LTD
IN A SPECIAL EDITION OF 1,000
© 1992 ROYAL DOULTON

**Note:** Produced exclusively for U.K.I. Ceramics Ltd. in a special edition of 1,000.

| *Back Stamp* | *U.S. $* | *Price Can. $* | *U.K. £* | *Aust. $* |
|---|---|---|---|---|
| BK-'Special' | 75.00 | 95.00 | 45.00 | 120.00 |

**DB128**
**CLOWN BUNNYKINS™**
**First Version**

Designer: Denise Andrews
Modeller: Warren Platt
Height: 4 1/4", 10.8 cm
Colour: White costume with black patterned costume, red square on trousers and red ruff at neck
Issued: 1992 (© 1992)
Varieties: DB 129

**Note:** Produced exclusively for U.K.I. Ceramics Ltd. in a special edition of 750

| *Back Stamp* | *U.S. $* | *Price Can. $* | *U.K. £* | *Aust. $* |
|---|---|---|---|---|
| BK-'Special' | 200.00 | 250.00 | 125.00 | 275.00 |

**DB129**
**CLOWN BUNNYKINS™**
**Second Version**

Designer: Denise Andrews
Modeller: Warren Platt
Height: 4 1/4", 10.8 cm
Colour: White costume with red patterned costume, black ruff around neck
Issued: 1992 (© 1992)
Varieties: DB 128

**Note:** Produced exclusively for U.K.I. Ceramics Ltd. in a special edition of 250.

| *Back Stamp* | *U.S. $* | *Price Can. $* | *U.K. £* | *Aust. $* |
|---|---|---|---|---|
| BK-'Special' | 500.00 | 600.00 | 450.00 | 650.00 |

**DB130**
**SWEETHEART BUNNYKINS™**

Designer: Graham Tongue
Modeller: Warren Platt
Height: 3 3/4", 9.5 cm
Colour: Yellow sweater, blue trousers, red heart
Issued: 1992-1992 (© 1992)

**Note:** Introduced at the International Collectables Exposition at South Bend, Indiana, July 1992

| *Back Stamp* | *U.S. $* | *Price Can. $* | *U.K. £* | *Aust. $* |
|---|---|---|---|---|
| BK-'Special' | 40.00 | 52.00 | 13.50 | 57.00 |

## DB131
## MASTER POTTER BUNNYKINS™

| | |
|---|---|
| Designer: | Graham Tongue |
| Modeller: | Warren Platt |
| Height: | 3 3/4", 9.3 cm |
| Colour: | Blue, white, green and brown |
| Issued: | 1993 - 1993 (© 1992) |
| Series: | RDICC |

**Note:** Produced exclusively for the Royal Doulton International Collectiors Club in 1993

| *Back Stamp* | *U.S. $* | *Price Can. $* | *U.K. £* | *Aust. $* |
|---|---|---|---|---|
| BK-'Special' | 100.00 | 100.00 | 45.00 | 89.00 |

## DB132
## HALLOWEEN BUNNYKINS™

| | |
|---|---|
| Designer: | Graham Tongue |
| Modeller: | Martyn Alcock |
| Height: | 3 1/4", 8.3 cm |
| Colour: | Orange and yellow pumpkin |
| Issued: | 1993 (© 1993) |

Note: Pre-released in U.S.A. in 1993

| *Back Stamp* | *U.S. $* | *Price Can $* | *U.K. £* | *Aust. $* |
|---|---|---|---|---|
| BK-5 | 50.00 | 75.00 | 20.00 | 79.00 |

## DB133
## AUSSIE SURFER BUNNYKINS™

| | |
|---|---|
| Designer: | Graham Tongue |
| Modeller: | Martyn Alcock |
| Height: | 4", 10.1 cm |
| Colour: | Gold and green outfir, white and blue base |
| Issued: | 1994 |

**Note:** Produced exclusively for Royal Doulton, Australia

| *Back Stamp* | *U.S. $* | *Price Can. $* | *U.K. £* | *Aust. $* |
|---|---|---|---|---|
| BK-'Special' | 75.00 | 75.00 | 30.00 | 79.00 |

**DB134**
**JOHN BULL BUNNYKINS™**

| | |
|---|---|
| Designer: | Denise Andrews |
| Modeller: | Amanda Hughes-Lubeck |
| Height: | 4 1/2", 11 cm |
| Colour: | Grey, yellow, red, white and blue Union Jack waistcoat |
| Issued: | 1993 (© 1993) |

**Note:** Produced exclusively for U.K. International Ceramics Ltd. in a Special Limited Edition of 1,000

| *Back Stamp* | *U.S. $* | *Price Can. $* | *U.K. £* | *Aust. $* |
|---|---|---|---|---|
| BK-'Special' | 75.00 | 100.00 | 45.00 | 110.00 |

**DB135**
**CONSTABLE MOUNTIE BUNNYKINS™**

| | |
|---|---|
| Designer: | Graham Tongue |
| Modeller: | Warren Platt |
| Height: | 4", 10.1 cm |
| Colour: | Red jacket, dark blue trousers and brown hat |
| Issued: | 1993 (© 1993) |

**Note:** Produced exclusively for the Doulton Collectors Weekend in Toronto during 1993 in a special edition of 750. "1873-1973 120 Years".

| *Back Stamp* | *U.S. $* | *Price Can. $* | *U.K. £* | *Aust. $* |
|---|---|---|---|---|
| BK-'Special' | 175.00 | 200.00 | 90.00 | 250.00 |

**DB136**
**SERGEANT MOUNTIE BUNNYKINS™**

| | |
|---|---|
| Designer: | Graham Tongue |
| Modeller: | Warren Platt |
| Height: | 4", 10.1 cm |
| Colour: | Red jacket, dark blue trouser, brown hat and yellow stripes |
| Issued: | 1993 (© 1993) |

**Note:** Produced exclusively for the Doulton Collectors Weekend in Toronto during 1993 in a special edition of 250. "1873-1993 120 Years"

| *Back Stamp* | *U.S. $* | *Price Can. $* | *U.K. £* | *Aust. $* |
|---|---|---|---|---|
| BK-'Special' | 500.00 | 700.00 | 350.00 | 600.00 |

**DB137**
**60TH ANNIVERSARY BUNNYKINS™**

Designer: Denise Andrews
Modeller: Warren Platt
Height: 4 1/2", 11 cm
Colour: Lemon, yellow and white
Issued: 1994 only

60th ANNIVERSARY
BUNNYKINS
DB 137
© 1993 ROYAL DOULTON

| *Back Stamp* | *U.S. $* | *Price Can. $* | *U.K. £* | *Aust. $* |
|---|---|---|---|---|
| BK-6 | 40.00 | 52.00 | 14.95 | 67.00 |

**DB142**
**CHEERLEADER BUNNYKINS™**

Designer: Denise Andrews
Modeller: Warren Platt
Height: 4 1/2", 11 cm
Colour: Red
Issued: 1994 by U.K. International Ceramics, Special Edition of 1,000

CHEERLEADER BUNNYKINS
DB 142
PRODUCED EXCLUSIVELY
FOR U.K.I. CERAMICS LTD
IN A SPECIAL EDITION OF 1,000
© 1994 ROYAL DOULTON
1994

| *Back Stamp* | *U.S. $* | *Price Can. $* | *U.K.* | *Aust. $* |
|---|---|---|---|---|
| BK-'Special' | 75.00 | 100.00 | 38.00 | 100.00 |

**DB143**
**CHEERLEADER BUNNYKINS™**

Designer: Denise Andrews
Modeller: Warren Platt
Height: 4 1/2", 11 cm
Colour: Yellow
Issued: 1994 by U.K. International Ceramics, Special Edition of 1, 000 for Doulton Fairs in England

CHEERLEADER BUNNYKINS
DB 143
PRODUCED EXCLUSIVELY
FOR U.K.I. CERAMICS LTD
DOULTON FAIRS
SPECIAL EDITION OF 1,000
© 1994 ROYAL DOULTON
1994

| *Back Stamp* | *U.S. $* | *Price Can. $* | *U.K.* | *Aust. $* |
|---|---|---|---|---|
| BK-'Special' | 75.00 | 100.00 | 38.00 | 100.00 |

**DB144**
**BATSMAN BUNNYKINS™**

Designer: Denise Andrews
Modeller: Amanda Hughes-Lubeck
Height: 4", 10.1 cm
Colour: White, beige and black
Issued: 1994 U.K. International Ceramics Ltd.
Special Edition of 1,000

| *Back Stamp* | *U.S. $* | *Price Can. $* | *U.K.* | *Aust. $* |
|---|---|---|---|---|
| BK-'Special' | 75.00 | 100.00 | 38.00 | 100.00 |

**DB145**
**BOWLER BUNNYKINS™**

Designer: Denise Andrews
Modeller: Warren Platt
Height: 4", 10.1 cm
Colour: White, beige and black
Issued: 1994 by U.K. International Ceramics Ltd.
Special Edition of 1,000

| *Back Stamp* | *U.S. $* | *Price Can. $* | *U.K.* | *Aust. $* |
|---|---|---|---|---|
| BK-'Special' | 75.00 | 100.00 | 38.00 | 100.00 |

**DB146**
**CHRISTMAS SURPRISE BUNNYKINS™**

Designer: Graham Tongue
Modeller: Warren Platt
Height: 3 1/2", 8.9 cm
Colour: Cream and Red
Issued: 1994 to the present

| *Back Stamp* | *U.S. $* | *Price Can. $* | *U.K. £* | *Aust. $* |
|---|---|---|---|---|
| BK-6 | 40.00 | 52.00 | 14.95 | 57.00 |

**DB147**
**RAINYDAY BUNNYKINS™**

| | |
|---|---|
| Designer: | Graham Tongue |
| Modeller: | Warren Platt |
| Height: | 4", 10.1 cm |
| Colour: | Yellow coat and hat, blue trouseres, black boots |
| Issued: | 1994 (© 1994) |

| *Back Stamp* | *U.S. $* | *Price Can. $* | *U.K. £* | *Aust. $* |
|---|---|---|---|---|
| BK-6 | 40.00 | 52.00 | 14.95 | 57.00 |

**DB148**
**BATHTIME BUNNYKINS™**

| | |
|---|---|
| Designer: | Graham Tongue |
| Modeller: | Warren Platt |
| Height: | 4", 10.1 cm |
| Colour: | White bathrobe with grey trim, yellow towel and duck |
| Issued: | 1994 (©1994) |

| *Back Stamp* | *U.S. $* | *Price Can. $* | *U.K. £* | *Aust. $* |
|---|---|---|---|---|
| BK-6 | 40.00 | 52.00 | 14.95 | 57.00 |

***Photograph Not Available at Press Time***

**DB149**
**EASTER GREETINGS BUNNYKINS™**

| | |
|---|---|
| Designer: | Graham Tongue |
| Modeller: | Warren Platt |
| Height: | Unknown |
| Colour: | Unknown |
| Issued: | 1995 by U.K. International Ceramics Ltd. |

| *Back Stamp* | *U.S. $* | *Price Can. $* | *U.K. £* | *Aust. $* |
|---|---|---|---|---|
| BK-'Special' | N/A | N/A | N/A | N/A |

**DB150**
**WICKET KEEPER™**

| | |
|---|---|
| Designer: | Denise Andrews |
| Modeller: | Amanda Hughes-Lubeck |
| Height: | 3 1/2", 8.9 cm |
| Colour: | White, beige and black |
| Issued: | 1995 by U.K. International Ceramics Ltd.<br>Special Edition of 1,000 |

| *Back Stamp* | *U.S. $* | *Price Can. $* | *U.K. £* | *Aust. $* |
|---|---|---|---|---|
| BK-6 Special | 75.00 | 100.00 | 38.00 | 100.00 |

**DB6966**
**CITY GENT TEAPOT™**

| | |
|---|---|
| Designer: | Unknown |
| Modeller: | Martyn Alcock |
| Height: | 8", 20.3 cm |
| Colour: | Brown bunny, black waist coat, hat and brolly,<br>green and white tie, black and white newspaper |
| Issued: | 1994 by John Sinclair, Sheffield<br>Limited Edition 2,500 |

**Note:** Royal Doulton original

| *Back Stamp* | *U.S. $* | *Price Can. $* | *U.K. £* | *Aust. $* |
|---|---|---|---|---|
| BK-D6966 | N/A | N/A | 50.00 | N/A |

*THE SNOWMAN*
*GIFT COLLECTION*

## DS 1
## JAMES™

Designer: Harry Sales
Modeller: David Lyttleton
Height: 3 3/4", 9.5 cm
Colour: Blue and white striped pyjamas brown dressing gown
Issued: 1985 - 1993

Royal Doulton®
THE SNOWMAN™
GIFT COLLECTION
JAMES
DS 1
© 1985 ROYAL DOULTON (UK)
© S ENT 1985

| Back Stamp | U.S. $ | Price Can. $ | U.K. £ | Aust. $ |
|---|---|---|---|---|
| DS-1 | 50.00 | 75.00 | 30.00 | 80.00 |

## DS 2
## THE SNOWMAN™

Designer: Harry Sales
Modeller: David Lyttleton
Height: 5", 12.7 cm
Colour: Green hat and scarf
Issued: 1985 to the present

Royal Doulton®
THE SNOWMAN™
GIFT COLLECTION
THE SNOWMAN
DS 2
© 1985 ROYAL DOULTON (UK)
© S ENT 1985

| Back Stamp | U.S. $ | Price Can. $ | U.K. £ | Aust. $ |
|---|---|---|---|---|
| DS-1 | 35.00 | 60.00 | 14.95 | 70.00 |

## DS 3
## STYLISH SNOWMAN™

Designer: Harry Sales
Modeller: David Lyttleton
Height: 5", 12.7 cm
Colour: Blue trousers, lilac braces, grey hat, yellow tie with red stripes.
Issued: 1985 - 1993
© 1985 R.D. (U.K.) © S.ENT.1985

Royal Doulton®
THE SNOWMAN™
GIFT COLLECTION
STYLISH SNOWMAN
DS 3
© 1985 ROYAL DOULTON (UK)
© S ENT 1985

| Back Stamp | U.S. $ | Price Can. $ | U.K. £ | Aust. $ |
|---|---|---|---|---|
| DS-1 | 35.00 | 60.00 | 14.00 | 60.00 |

**DS 4**
**THANK YOU SNOWMAN™**

| | |
|---|---|
| Designer: | Harry Sales |
| Modeller: | David Lyttleton |
| Height: | 5", 12.7 cm |
| Colour: | Snowman has green hat and scarf; James wears a brown dressing gown |
| Issued: | 1985 to the present |

© 1985 R.D. (U.K.) © S.ENT.1985

| *Back Stamp* | *U.S. $* | *Price Can. $* | *U.K. £* | *Aust. $* |
|---|---|---|---|---|
| DS-1 | 45.00 | 65.00 | 19.95 | 60.00 |

**DS 5**
**SNOWMAN MAGIC - MUSIC BOX™**

| | |
|---|---|
| Designer: | Harry Sales |
| Modeller: | David Lyttleton |
| Height: | 8", 20.3 cm |
| Colour: | Cream music box with blue, green and pink balloon design |
| Issued: | 1985 to the present<br>© 1985 R.D. (U.K.) © S.ENT.1985 |
| Tune: | "Walking in the Air" |

| *Back Stamp* | *U.S. $* | *Price Can. $* | *U.K. £* | *Aust. $* |
|---|---|---|---|---|
| DS-1 | 65.00 | 85.00 | 29.95 | 100.00 |

*Photograph Not Available at Press Time*

**DS 6**
**COWBOY SNOWMAN™**

| | |
|---|---|
| Designer: | Harry Sales |
| Modeller: | David Lyttleton |
| Height: | 5", 12.7 cm |
| Colour: | Brown hat and holster belt |
| Issued: | 1986 - 1992<br>© 1985 R.D. (U.K.) © S.ENT.1985 |

| *Back Stamp* | *U.S. $* | *Price Can. $* | *U.K. £* | *Aust. $* |
|---|---|---|---|---|
| DS-1 | 45.00 | 65.00 | 30.00 | 60.00 |

**DS 7**
**HIGHLAND SNOWMAN™**

| | |
|---|---|
| Designer: | Harry Sales |
| Modeller: | David Lyttleton |
| Height: | 5 1/4", 13.3 cm |
| Colour: | Red, blue and white kilt |
| Issued: | 1987 - 1993 |

Royal Doulton®
THE SNOWMAN™
GIFT COLLECTION
HIGHLAND SNOWMAN
DS 7
© 1985 ROYAL DOULTON (UK)
© S. ENT 1985

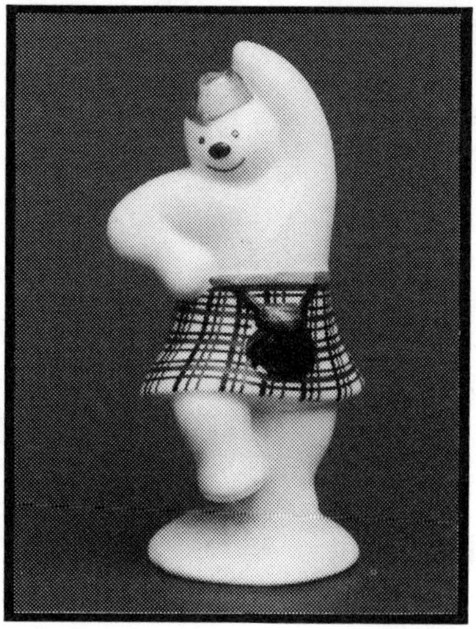

| *Back Sstamp* | *U.S. $* | *Price Can. $* | *U.K. £* | *Aust. $* |
|---|---|---|---|---|
| DS-1 | 35.00 | 50.00 | 25.00 | 60.00 |

**DS 8**
**LADY SNOWMAN™**

| | |
|---|---|
| Designer: | Harry Sales |
| Modeller: | David Lyttleton |
| Height: | 5", 12.7 cm |
| Colour: | Pink apron, blue hat |
| Issued: | 1987 - 1992 |

Royal Doulton®
THE SNOWMAN™
GIFT COLLECTION
LADY SNOWMAN
DS 8
© 1985 ROYAL DOULTON (UK)
© S ENT 1985

| *Back Stamp* | *U.S. $* | *Price Can. $* | *U.K. £* | *Aust. $* |
|---|---|---|---|---|
| DS-1 | 50.00 | 70.00 | 35.00 | 60.00 |

**DS 9**
**BASS DRUMMER SNOWMAN™**

| | |
|---|---|
| Designer: | Graham Tongue |
| Modeller: | Warren Platt |
| Height: | 5 1/2", 13.3 cm |
| Colour: | Pink and yellow drum, brown straps; pale blue hat |
| Issued: | 1987 - 1993 |
| | © 1987 R.D. © S.ENT. 1987 |

Royal Doulton®
THE SNOWMAN™
GIFT COLLECTION
BASS DRUMMER SNOWMAN
DS 9
© 1987 ROYAL DOULTON
© S ENT 1987

| *Back Stamp* | *U.S. $* | *Price Can. $* | *U.K. £* | *Aust. $* |
|---|---|---|---|---|
| DS-1 | 40.00 | 50.00 | 25.00 | 60.00 |

**DS 10**
**FLAUTIST SNOWMAN™**

Designer: Graham Tongue
Modeller: Warren Platt
Height: 5 1/2", 14.0 cm
Colour: Yellow and red cap, brown tie
Issued: 1987 - 1993
© 1987 Royal Doulton © S. ENT 1987

Royal Doulton®
THE SNOWMAN™
GIFT COLLECTION
FLAUTIST SNOWMAN
DS 10
© 1987 ROYAL DOULTON
© S. ENT 1987

| *Back Stamp* | *U.S. $* | *Price Can. $* | *U.K. £* | *Aust. $* |
|---|---|---|---|---|
| DS-1 | 40.00 | 50.00 | 25.00 | 60.00 |

**DS 11**
**VIOLINIST SNOWMAN™**

Royal Doulton®
THE SNOWMAN™
GIFT COLLECTION
VIOLINIST SNOWMAN
DS 11
© 1987 ROYAL DOULTON
© S. ENT 1987

Designer: Graham Tongue
Modeller: Warren Platt
Height: 5 1/4", 13.3 cm
Colour: Green waistcoat with yellow collar, brown cap and violin, blue bow tie
Issued: 1987 to the present
© 1988 Royal Doulton © S. ENT 1988

| *Back Stamp* | *U.S. $* | *Price Can. $* | *U.K. £* | *Aust. $* |
|---|---|---|---|---|
| DS-1 | 42.00 | 55.00 | 14.95 | 60.00 |

**DS 12**
**PIANIST SNOWMAN™**

Designer: Graham Tongue
Modeller: Warren Platt
Height: 5", 12.7 cm
Colour: Blue crown, orange tie
Issued: 1987 to the present

Royal Doulton®
THE SNOWMAN™
GIFT COLLECTION
PIANIST SNOWMAN
DS 12
© 1987 ROYAL DOULTON
© S. ENT 1987

| *Back Stamp* | *U.S. $* | *Price Can. $* | *U.K. £* | *Aust. $* |
|---|---|---|---|---|
| DS-1 | 45.00 | 60.00 | 20.00 | 85.00 |

## DS 13
## SNOWMAN'S PIANO™

Designer: Graham Tongue
Modeller: Warren Platt
Height: 5", 13.3 cm
Colour: White
Issued: 1987 to the present

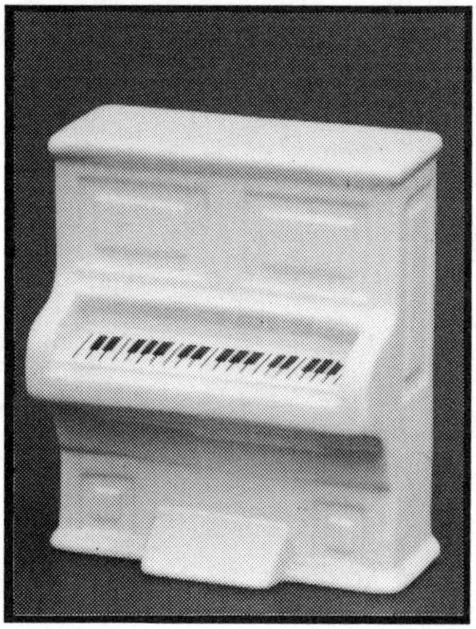

| *Back Sstamp* | *U.S. $* | *Price Can. $* | *U.K. £* | *Aust. $* |
|---|---|---|---|---|
| DS-1 | 45.00 | 60.00 | 14.95 | 60.00 |

## DS 14
## CYMBAL PLAYER SNOWMAN™

Designer: Graham Tongue
Modeller: Warren Platt
Height: 5 1/4", 13.3 cm
Colour: Brown waistcoat, green cap and bow tie, yellow cymbals
Issued: 1988 - 1993
© 1988 Royal Doulton © S. ENT 1988

| *Back Sstamp* | *U.S. $* | *Price Can. $* | *U.K. £* | *Aust. $* |
|---|---|---|---|---|
| DS-1 | 40.00 | 50.00 | 25.00 | 60.00 |

## DS 15
## DRUMMER SNOWMAN™

Designer: Graham Tongue
Modeller: Warren Platt
Height: 5 3/4", 14.6 cm
Colour: Red and black hat, purple bow tie, pink and yellow drum
Issued: 1988 to the present
© 1988 Royal Doulton © S. ENT 1988

| *Back Stamp* | *U.S. $* | *Price Can. $* | *U.K. £* | *Aust. $* |
|---|---|---|---|---|
| DS-1 | 35.00 | 50.00 | 14.95 | 60.00 |

## DS 16
## TRUMPETER SNOWMAN™

| | |
|---|---|
| Designer: | Graham Tongue |
| Modeller: | Warren Platt |
| Height: | 5", 12.7 cm |
| Colour: | Pink hat, yellow trumpet |
| Issued: | 1988-1993 |
| | © 1988 Royal Doulton © S. ENT 1988 |

| *Back Stamp* | *U.S. $* | *Price Can. $* | *U.K. £* | *Aust. $* |
|---|---|---|---|---|
| DS-1 | 40.00 | 50.00 | 25.00 | 60.00 |

## DS 17
## CELLIST SNOWMAN™

| | |
|---|---|
| Designer: | Graham Tongue |
| Modeller: | Warren Platt |
| Height: | 5 1/4", 13.3 cm |
| Colour: | Green waistcoat with yellow collar, brown coat and cello, blue bow tie |
| Issued: | 1988 - 1993 |

| *Back Stamp* | *U.S. $* | *Price Can. $* | *U.K. £* | *Aust. $* |
|---|---|---|---|---|
| DS-1 | 42.00 | 50.00 | 14.95 | 70.00 |

***Photograph Not Available at Press Time***

## DS 18
## SNOWMAN MUSICAL BOX™

| | |
|---|---|
| Designer: | Unknown |
| Height: | Unknown |
| Colour: | Unknown |
| Issued: | 1988 - 1990 |

Tune - Blue Bells of Scotland

| *Back Sstamp* | *U.S. $* | *Price Can. $* | *U.K. £* | *Aust. $* |
|---|---|---|---|---|
| DS-1 | 40.00 | 50.00 | 14.95 | 60.00 |

**DS 19**
**SNOWMAN MONEY BOX™**

| | |
|---|---|
| Designer: | Graham Tongue |
| Modeller: | Warren Platt |
| Height: | 8 1/2", 21.6 cm |
| Colour: | Green hat and scarf with grey band |
| Issued: | 1990 to the present |
| | © 1990 Royal Doulton © S. ENT 1990 |

| *Back Stamp* | *U.S. $* | *Price Can. $* | *U.K. £* | *Aust. $* |
|---|---|---|---|---|
| DS-1 | 35.00 | 55.00 | 15.00 | 70.00 |

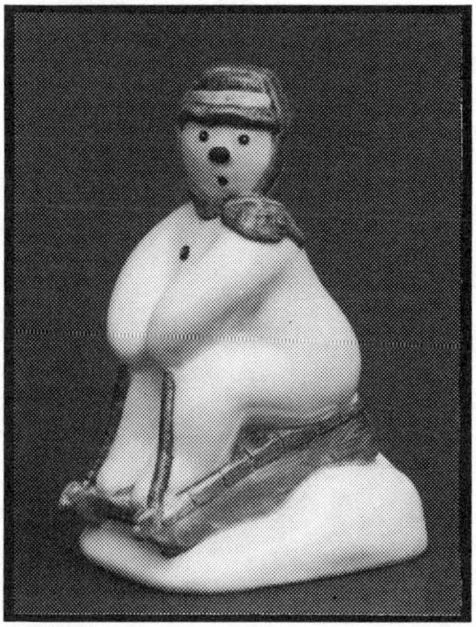

**DS 20**
**THE SNOWMAN TOBOGGANING™**

| | |
|---|---|
| Designer: | Graham Tongue |
| Modeller: | Warren Platt |
| Height: | 5", 12.7 cm |
| Colour: | Green hat and scarf, rose-pink toboggan |
| Issued: | 1990 to the present |
| | © 1990 Royal Doulton © S. ENT 1990 |

Royal Doulton®
THE SNOWMAN™
GIFT COLLECTION
THE SNOWMAN
TOBOGGANING
DS 20
© 1990 ROYAL DOULTON
© S ENT 1990

| *Back Stamp* | *U.S. $* | *Price Can. $* | *U.K. £* | *Aust. $* |
|---|---|---|---|---|
| DS-1 | 35.00 | 50.00 | 15.00 | 65.00 |

**DS 21**
**THE SNOWMAN SKIING™**

| | |
|---|---|
| Designer: | Graham Tongue |
| Modeller: | Warren Platt |
| Height: | 5", 12.7 cm |
| Colour: | Green hat and scarf, yellow and black goggles |
| Issued: | 1990 - 1992 |

Royal Doulton®
THE SNOWMAN™
GIFT COLLECTION
THE SNOWMAN
SKIING
DS 21
© 1990 ROYAL DOULTON
© S. ENT 1990

| *Back Stamp* | *U.S. $* | *Price Can. $* | *U.K. £* | *Aust. $* |
|---|---|---|---|---|
| DS-1 | 50.00 | 60.00 | 30.00 | 80.00 |

**DS 22**
**THE SNOWBALLING SNOWMAN™**

| | |
|---|---|
| Designer: | Graham Tongue |
| Modeller: | Warren Platt |
| Height: | 5", 12.7 cm |
| Colour: | Green had and scarf, brown tree stump |
| Issued: | 1990 to the present |

| *Back Stamp* | *U.S. $* | *Price Can. $* | *U.K. £* | *Aust. $* |
|---|---|---|---|---|
| DS1 | 50.00 | 60.00 | 15.00 | 80.00 |

**DS 23**
**BUILDING THE SNOWMAN™**

| | |
|---|---|
| Designer: | Graham Tongue |
| Modeller: | Warren Platt |
| Height: | 4", 10.1 cm |
| Colour: | Green hat and scarf |
| Issued: | 1990 to the present |
| | © 1900 Royal Doulton © S.ENT 1990 |

Royal Doulton®
THE SNOWMAN™
GIFT COLLECTION
BUILDING THE
SNOWMAN
DS 23
© 1990 ROYAL DOULTON
© S.ENT 1990

| *Back Stamp* | *U.S. $* | *Price Can. $* | *U.K. £* | *Aust.* |
|---|---|---|---|---|
| DS1 | 42.00 | 60.00 | 15.00 | 80.00 |

**D6972**
**SNOWMAN MINIATURE CHARACTER JUG™**

| | |
|---|---|
| Designer: | Graham Tongue |
| Modeller: | Martyn Alcock |
| Height: | 2 3/4", 7.0 cm |
| Colour: | White |
| Issued: | 1994 to the present |

| *Back Stamp* | *U.S. $* | *Can. $* | *Price U.K. £* | *Aust. $* |
|---|---|---|---|---|
| DS1 | 50.00 | 75.00 | 19.95 | 75.00 |

# *INDICES*

# BUYING and SELLING ROYAL DOULTON

***...is easy!***

Collecting **Royal Doulton** is really fun. For many collectors it has turned into a great investment as well, as they have watched the value of their collection grow. From time to time for many reasons, collectors wish to **buy, sell** or **trade** certain portions or their entire collection. Many of these collectors in the United States and Canada turn to *Seaway China.* From both countries we are only a toll free call away at

**1-800-968-2424**

**WHERE TO SELL ROYAL DOULTON**

## Seaway China Company

*"INTERNATIONAL ROYAL DOULTON SPECIALISTS"*

102 Broadway, Marine City, MI. U.S.A. 48039-1702

**1-800-968-2424**

# Royal Doulton News

Marine City, MI, 1994

## Beatrix Potter and Bunnykins - A Specialty At *Seaway China*

...When you have a store full of Royal Doulton - from the front door to the back room -- you have room for a lot of little characters. These little characters are of course the little characters from those world famous Beatrix Potter stories.

At Seaway China they have a very special home that they share with one of worlds largest collections of Bunnykins.

The gang at Seaway China pay special attention to all the old, current and recent releases of both Beatrix Potter and Bunnykins.

When you wish to add to your collection, give the gang at Seaway China a call. You can reach them from anywhere in the United States or Canada at 1-800-968-2424.

Seaway accepts all major credit cards and can usually ship orders the same day.

## Real Dog on Guard at Royal Doulton Store

"Mindy", a purebred Pomeranian, works at Seaway China Shop every day. When awake she serves as "guard dog" to the giant Seaway collection of Royal Doulton animals, character jugs and figurines. As international as Royal Doulton itself, Mindy is a native of Florida, lives in Canada and works in the Michigan, U.S.A. shop daily. Drop in and meet her.

Mindy has agreed to let her picture appear to represent all the real pets who serve as priceless companions to their masters who are Royal Doulton collectors.

*Santa Tiny - New for 1994*

## Second Santa Tiny Ready for 1994.

Marine City, USA

Seaway China of Marine City, Michigan have announced that their second Santa Claus Tiny character jug will be ready for the 1994 Christmas Season.

First in the series, the Tiny Santa Claus character jug, with a regular red handle is now over 80% Sold Out. Second in the series of three is Santa Claus with a red and white candy cane handle.

Seaway China is accepting orders for both character jugs at 1-800-968-2424.

# ALPHABETICAL INDEX OF FIGURES

## *ALPHABETICAL INDEX TO BESWICK MODEL NUMBERS FOR BEATRIX POTTER FIGURES*

### H

| | |
|---|---|
| Hunca Munca | 1198 |
| Hunca Munca Spills the Beads | 3288 |
| Hunca Munca Sweeping | 2584 |

### J

| | |
|---|---|
| Jemima Puddle-Duck (First Version) | 1092/1 |
| Jemima Puddle-Duck (Second Version) | 1092/2 |
| Jemima Puddle-Duck Character Jug | ?? |
| Jemima Puddle-Duck and Foxy Whiskered Gentleman | 3193 |
| Jemima Puddle-Duck and Foxy Whiskered Gentleman Plaque | 2594 |
| Jemima Puddle-Duck Made a Feather Nest | 2823 |
| Jemima Puddle-Duck Plaque | 2082 |
| John Joiner | 2965 |
| Johnny Town-Mouse | 1276 |
| Johnny Town-Mouse with Bag | 3094 |

### L

| | |
|---|---|
| Lady Mouse | 1183 |
| Lady Mouse Made a Curtsey | 3220 |
| Little Black Rabbit | 2585 |
| Little Pig Robinson (First Version) | 1104/1 |
| Little Pig Robinson (Second Version) | 1104/2 |
| Little Pig Robinson Spying | 3031 |

### M

| | |
|---|---|
| Miss Dormouse | 3251 |
| Miss Moppet (First Version) | 1275/1 |
| Miss Moppet (Second Version) | 1275/2 |
| Mittens and Moppet | 3197 |
| Mother Ladybird | 2966 |
| Mr. Alderman Ptolemy | 2424 |
| Mr. Benjamin Bunny (First Version) | 1940/1 |
| Mr. Benjamin Bunny (Second Version) | 1940/2 |
| Mr. Benjamin Bunny and Peter Rabbit | 2509 |
| Mr. Drake Puddle-Duck | 2628 |
| Mr. Jackson (First Version) | 2453/1 |
| Mr. Jackson (Second Version) | 2453/2 |
| Mr. Jeremy Fisher (First Version) | 1157/1 |
| Mr. Jeremy Fisher (Second Version) | 1157/2 |
| Mr. Jeremy Fisher (Third Version - large) | 1157/3 |
| Mr. Jeremy Fisher Character Jug | |
| Mr. Jeremy Fisher Digging | 3090 |
| Mr. Tod | 3091 |
| Mrs. Flopsy Bunny | 1942 |
| Mrs. Rabbit (First Version) | 1200/1 |
| Mrs. Rabbit (Second Version) | 1200/2 |
| Mrs. Rabbit (Third Version - large) | 1200/3 |
| Mrs. Rabbit and Bunnies | 2543 |
| Mrs. Rabbit Cooking | 3278 |
| Mrs. Tiggy-Winkle (First Version) | 1107/1 |
| Mrs. Tiggy-Winkle (Second Version) | 1107/2 |
| Mrs. Tiggy-Winkle Character Jug | 3102 |
| Mrs. Tiggy-Winkle Takes Tea | 2877 |
| Mrs. Tittlemouse | 1103 |
| Mrs. Tittlemouse Plaque | 2685 |

### N

| | |
|---|---|
| No More Twist | 3325 |

### O

| | |
|---|---|
| Old Mr. Bouncer | 2956 |
| Old Mr. Brown | 1796 |
| Old Mr. Brown Character Jug | |
| Old Mr. Pricklepin | 2767 |

### P

| | |
|---|---|
| Peter and the Red Pocket Handkerchief | 3242 |
| Peter Rabbit (First Version) | 1098/1 |
| Peter Rabbit (Second Version) | 1098/2 |
| Peter Rabbit (Third Version - large) | 1098/3 |
| Peter Rabbit Character Jug | |
| Peter Rabbit in the Gooseberry Net | 3157 |
| Peter Rabbit Plaque (First Version) | 2083 |
| Peter Rabbit Plaque (Second Version) | 2650 |
| Pickles | 2334 |
| Pigling Bland (First Version) | 1365/1 |
| Pigling Bland (Second Version) | 1365/2 |
| Pigling Eats his Porridge | 3252 |
| Pig-Wig | 2381 |
| Poorly Peter Rabbit | 2560 |

### R

| | |
|---|---|
| Rebeccah Puddle-Duck | 2647 |
| Ribby | 1199 |
| Ribby and the Patty Pan | 3280 |

### S

| | |
|---|---|
| Sally Henny Penny (First Version) | 2452/1 |
| Sally Henny Penny (Second Version) | 2452/2 |
| Samuel Whiskers | 1106 |
| Simpkin | 2508 |
| Sir Isaac Newton | 2425 |
| Squirrel Nutkin (First Version) | 1102/1 |
| Squirrel Nutkin (Second Version) | 1102/2 |
| Susan | 2716 |

### T

| | |
|---|---|
| Tabitha Twitchet (First Version) | 1676/1 |
| Tabitha Twitchet (Second Version) | 1676/2 |
| Tabitha Twitchet and Miss Moppet | 2544 |
| Tailor of Gloucester | 1108 |
| The Old Woman who Lived in a Shoe | 1545 |
| The Old Woman who Lived in a Shoe Knitting | 2804 |
| Thomasina Tittlemouse | 2668 |
| Timmy Tiptoes (First Version) | 1101/1 |
| Timmy Tiptoes (Second Version) | 1101/2 |
| Timmy Willie from Johnny Town-Mouse | 1109 |
| Timmy Willie Sleeping | 2996 |
| Tom Kitten (First Version) | 1100/1 |
| Tom Kitten (Second Version) | 1100/2 |
| Tom Kitten (Third Version - large) | 1100/3 |
| Tom Kitten and Butterfly | 3030 |
| Tom Kitten Character Jug | |
| Tom Kitten Plaque | 2085 |
| Tom Thumb | 2989 |
| Tommy Brock (First Version) | 1348/1 |
| Tommy Brock (Second Version) | 1348/2 |
| Tommy Brock (Third Verson) | 1348/3 |
| Tommy Brock (Fourth Version) | 1348/4 |
| Tree Lamp Base | 1531 |

# *ALPHABETICAL INDEX TO ROYAL DOULTON BRAMBLY HEDGE NUMBERS (DBH) FOR BRAMBLY HEDGE FIGURES*

# ALPHBETICAL INDEX TO ROYAL DOULTON BUNNYKINS NUMBERS (DB) FOR BUNNYKINS FIGURES

## A

| | |
|---|---|
| Ace Bunnykins | DB42 |
| Aerobic Bunnykins | DB40 |
| Astro Bunnykins Rocket Man | DB20 |
| Astro Bunnykins Rocket Man Music Box | DB35 |
| Aussie Surfer Bunnykins | DB133 |
| Australian Bunnykins | DB58 |

## B

| | |
|---|---|
| Bathtime Bunnykins | DB148 |
| Batsman Bunnykins | DB144 |
| Be Prepared Bunnykins | DB56 |
| Bedtime Bunnykins (First Version) | DB55 |
| Bedtime Bunnykins (Second Version) | DB63 |
| Bedtime Bunnykins (Third Version) | DB79 |
| Bedtime Bunnykins (Fourth Version) | DB103 |
| Billie And Buntie Bunnykins Sleigh Ride (First Version) | DB4 |
| Billie And Buntie Bunnykins Sleigh Ride (Second Version) | DB81 |
| Billie Bunnykins Cooling Off | DB3 |
| Billy Bunnykins | D6001 |
| Bogey Bunnykins | DB32 |
| Bowler Bunnykins | DB145 |
| Bride Bunnykins | DB101 |
| Brownie Bunnykins | DB61 |
| Bunny Bank (First Version) | D6615A |
| Bunny Bank (Second Version) | D6615B |
| Buntie Bunnykins Helping Mother | DB2 |
| Busy Needles Bunnykins | DB10 |

## C

| | |
|---|---|
| Carol Singer Bunnykins | DB104 |
| Carol Singer Music Box | DB53 |
| Cheerleader Bunnykins (First Version) | DB142 |
| Cheerleader Bunnykins (Second Version) | DB143 |
| Christmas Surprise Bunnykins | DB146 |
| City Gent Tea Pot | |
| Clown Bunnykins (First Version) | DB128 |
| Clown Bunnykins (Second Version) | DB129 |
| Collector Bunnykins | DB54 |
| Constable Mountie Bunnykins | DB135 |
| Cook Bunnykins | DB85 |
| Cymbals Bunnykins (First Version) | DB25 |
| Cymbals Bunnykins From The Oompah Band (Second Version) | DB88 |
| Cymbals Bunnykins From The Oompah Band(Third Version) | DB107 |

## D

| | |
|---|---|
| Daisie Bunnykins Springtime | DB7 |
| Dollie Bunnykins Playtime (First Version) | DB8 |
| Dollie Bunnykins Playtime (Second Version) | DB80 |
| Downhill Bunnykins | DB31 |
| Drum-major Bunnykins (First Version) | DB27 |
| Drum-major Bunnykins (Second Version) | DB90 |
| Drum-major Bunnykins From The Oompah Band (Third Version) | DB109 DB109 |
| Drummer Bunnykins (Fourth Version) | DB108 |
| Drummer Bunnykins Bunnykins, Oompah Band Edition (First Version) | DB26 |
| Drummer Bunnykins 50th Anniversary Edition (Second Version) | DB26B |
| Drummer Bunnykins (Third Version) | DB89 |

## E

| | |
|---|---|
| Easter Greetings Bunnykins | DB149 |

## F

| | |
|---|---|
| Family Photograph Bunnykins (First Version) | DB1 |
| Family Photograph (Second Version) | DB67 |
| Farmer Bunnykins | D6003 |
| Father, Mother And Victoria Bunnykins | DB68 |
| Fireman Bunnykins | DB75 |
| Fisherman Bunnykins | DB84 |
| Footballer Bunnykins (First Version) | DB117 |
| Footballer Bunnykins (Second Version) | DB119 |
| Footballer Bunnykins (Third Version) | DB121 |
| Freddie Bunnykins | D6024 |
| Freefall Bunnykins | DB41 |

## G

| | |
|---|---|
| Goalkeeper Bunnykins (First Version ) | DB116 |
| Goalkeeper Bunnykins (Second Version) | DB118 |
| Goalkeeper Bunnykins (Third Version) | DB120 |
| Goalkeeper Bunnykins (Fourth Version) | DB122 |
| Grandpa's Story Bunnykins | DB14 |
| Groom Bunnykins | DB102 |
| Guardsman Bunnykins | DB127 |

## H

| | |
|---|---|
| Halloween Bunnykins | DB132 |
| Happy Birthday Bunnykins | DB21 |
| Happy Birthday Bunnykins Music Box | DB36 |
| Harry Bunnykins | DB73 |
| Harry The Herald (First Version) | DB49 |
| Harry The Herald (Second Version ) | DB95 |
| Harry The Herald (Third Version) | DB115 |
| Home Run Bunnykins (1 On Back Of Jersey) | DB43 |

## I

| | |
|---|---|
| Ice Cream Bunnykins | DB82 |

## J

| | |
|---|---|
| Jogging Bunnykins | DB22 |
| Jogging Bunnykins Music Box | DB37 |
| John Bull Bunnykins | DB134 |

*K*

| | |
|---|---|
| King John (First Version) | DB45 |
| King John (Second Version) | DB91 |
| Knockout Bunnykins | DB30 |

*L*

| | |
|---|---|
| Lollipopman Bunnykins | DB65 |

*M*

| | |
|---|---|
| Magician Bunnykins | DB126 |
| Mary Bunnykins | D6002 |
| Master Potter Bunnykins | DB131 |
| Milkman Bunnykins | DB125 |
| Mother Bunnykins | D6004 |
| Mr. Bunnybeat Strumming | DB16 |
| Mr. Bunnybeat Strumming Music Box | DB38 |
| Mr. Bunnykins At The Easter Parade (First Version) | DB18 |
| Mr. Bunnykins At The Easter Parade (Second Version) | DB51 |
| Mr. Bunnykins Autumn Days | DB5 |
| Mrs. Bunnykins At The East Parade Music Box | DB39 |
| Mrs. Bunnykins At The Easter Parade (First Version) | DB19 |
| Mrs. Bunnykins At The Easter Parade (Second Version) | DB52 |
| Mrs. Bunnykins Clean Sweep | DB6 |

*N*

| | |
|---|---|
| Nurse Bunnykins (First Version) | DB74A |
| Nurse Bunnykins (Second Version) | DB74B |

*O*

| | |
|---|---|
| Olympic Bunnykins (First Version) | DB28A |
| Olympic Bunnykins (Second Version) | DB28B |

*P*

| | |
|---|---|
| Paperboy Bunnykins | DB77 |
| Policeman Bunnykins | DB64 |
| Polly Bunnykins | DB71 |
| Postman Bunnykins | DB76 |
| Prince Frederick (First Version) | DB48 |
| Prince Frederick (Second Version) | DB94 |
| Princess Beatrice (First Version) | DB47 |
| Princess Beatrice (Second Version) | DB93 |

*Q*

| | |
|---|---|
| Queen Sophie (First Version) | DB46 |
| Queen Sophie (Second Version) | DB92 |

*R*

| | |
|---|---|
| Rainy Day Bunnykins | DB147 |
| Reggie Bunnykins | D6025 |
| Rise And Shine Bunnykins | DB11 |
| Rock 'n' Roll Bunnykins | DB124 |

*S*

| | |
|---|---|
| Santa Bunnykins Happy Christmas, Christmas Tree Ornament | DB62 |
| Santa Bunnykins Happy Christmas | DB17 |
| Santa Bunnykins Music Box | DB34 |
| School Days Bunnykins | DB57 |
| Schoolboy Bunnykins | DB66 |
| Schoolmaster Bunnykins | DB60 |
| Sergeant Mountie Bunnykins | DB136 |
| 60th Anniversary Bunnykins | DB137 |
| Sleepytime Bunnykins | DB15 |
| Soccer Player Bunnykins | DB123 |
| Sousaphone Bunnykins (First Version) | DB23 |
| Sousaphone Bunnykins From The Oompah Band (Second Version) | DB86 |
| Sousaphone Bunnykins From The Oompah Band (Third Version) | DB105 |
| Storytime Bunnykins (First Version) | DB9 |
| Storytime Bunnykins (Second Version) | DB59 |
| Susan Bunnykins As Queen Of The May | DB83 |
| Susan Bunnykins | DB70 |
| Sweetheart Bunnykins | DB130 |

*T*

| | |
|---|---|
| Tally Ho! Bunnykins (First Version) | DB12 |
| Tally Ho! Bunnykins (Second Version) | DB78 |
| Tally Ho! Music Box (First Version) | DB33A |
| Tally Ho! Music Box (Second Version) | DB33B |
| The Artist | DB13 |
| Tom Bunnykins | DB72 |
| Touchdown Bunnykins (First Version) | DB29A |
| Touchdown Bunnykins (Second Version) | DB29B |
| Touchdown Bunnykins Ohio State University (Third Version) | DB96 |
| Touchdown Bunnykins University Of Michigan (Fourth Version) | DB97 |
| Touchdown Bunnykins Cincinnati Bengals (Fifth Version) | DB98 |
| Touchdown Bunnykins Notre Dame College (Sixth Version) | DB99 |
| Touchdown Bunnykins University Of Indiana (Seventh Version) | DB100 |
| Trumpeter Bunnykins (First Version) | DB24 |
| Trumpeter Bunnykins From The Oompah Band (Second Version) | DB76 |
| Trumpeter Bunnykins From The Oompah Band (Third Version) | DB106 |

*U*

| | |
|---|---|
| Uncle Sam Bunnykins | DB50 |

*W*

| | |
|---|---|
| Wicket Keeper Bunnykins | DB150 |
| William Bunnykins | DB69 |

## ALPHABETICAL INDEX TO ROYAL DOULTON SNOWMAN NUMBERS (DS) FOR THE SNOWMEN FIGURES

### B

| | |
|---|---|
| Bass Drummer Snowman | DS9 |
| Building The Snowman | DS23 |

### C

| | |
|---|---|
| Cellist Snowman | DS17 |
| Cowboy Snowman | DS6 |
| Cymbal Player Snowman | DS14 |

### D

| | |
|---|---|
| Drummer Snowman | DS15 |

### F

| | |
|---|---|
| Flautist Snowman | DS10 |

### H

| | |
|---|---|
| Highland Snowman | DS7 |

### J

| | |
|---|---|
| James | DS1 |

### L

| | |
|---|---|
| Lady Snowman | DS8 |

### P

| | |
|---|---|
| Pianist Snowman | DS12 |

### S

| | |
|---|---|
| Snowman Miniature Character Jug | D6972 |
| Snowman Magic - Music Box | DS5 |
| Snowman's Musical Box | DS18 |
| Snowman's Money Box | DS19 |
| Snowman's Piano | DS13 |
| Snowman Snowballing | DS18 |
| Stylish Snowman | DS3 |

### T

| | |
|---|---|
| Thank You Snowman | DS4 |
| The Snowballing Snowman | DS22 |
| The Snowman | DS2 |
| The Snowman Skiing | DS21 |
| The Snowman Tobogganing | DS20 |
| Trumpeter Snowman | DS16 |

### V

| | |
|---|---|
| Violinist Snowman | DS11 |

## NUMERICAL INDEX TO BESWICK MODEL NUMBERS FOR BEATRIX POTTER FIGURES

| | |
|---|---|
| 1092/1 | Jemima Puddle-Duck (First Version) |
| 1092/2 | Jemima Puddle-Duck (Second Version) |
| 1098/1 | Peter Rabbit (First Version) |
| 1098/2 | Peter Rabbit (Second Version) |
| 1098/3 | Peter Rabbit (Third Version - large) |
| 1100/1 | Tom Kitten (First Version) |
| 1100/2 | Tom Kitten (Second Version) |
| 1100/3 | Tom Kitten (Third Version - large) |
| 1101/1 | Timmy Tiptoes (First Version) |
| 1101/2 | Timmy Tiptoes (Second Version) |
| 1102/1 | Squirrel Nutkin (First Version) |
| 1102/2 | Squirrel Nutkin (Second Version) |
| 1103 | Mrs. Tittlemouse |
| 1104/1 | Little Pig Robinson (First Version) |
| 1104/2 | Little Pig Robinson (Second Version) |
| 1105/1 | Benjamin Bunny (First Version) |
| 1105/2 | Benjamin Bunny (Second Version) |
| 1105/3 | Benjamin Bunny (Third Version) |
| 1105/4 | Benjamin Bunny (Fourth Version - large) |
| 1106 | Samuel Whiskers |
| 1107/1 | Mrs. Tiggy-Winkle (First Version) |
| 1107/2 | Mrs. Tiggy-Winkle (Second Version) |
| 1108 | Tailor of Gloucester |
| 1109 | Timmy Willie from Johnny Town-Mouse |
| 1157/1 | Mr. Jeremy Fisher (First Version) |
| 1157/2 | Mr. Jeremy Fisher (Second Version) |
| 1157/3 | Mr. Jeremy Fisher (Third Version - large) |
| 1183 | Lady Mouse |
| 1198 | Hunca Munca |
| 1199 | Ribby |
| 3280 | Ribby and the Patty Pan |
| 1200/1 | Mrs. Rabbit (First Version) |
| 1200/2 | Mrs. Rabbit (Second Version) |
| 1200/3 | Mrs. Rabbit (Third Version - large) |
| 1274 | Flopsy, Mopsy and Cottontail |
| 1275/1 | Miss Moppet (First Version) |
| 1275/2 | Miss Moppet (Second Version) |
| 1276 | Johnny Town-Mouse |
| 1277 | Foxy Whiskered Gentleman |
| 1348/1 | Tommy Brock (First Version) |

| | |
|---|---|
| 1348/2 | Tommy Brock (Second Version) |
| 1348/3 | Tommy Brock (Third Verson) |
| 1348/4 | Tommy Brock (Fourth Version) |
| 1355 | Duchess (Style One) |
| 1365/1 | Pigling Bland (First Version) |
| 1365/2 | Pigling Bland (Second Version) |
| 1531 | Tree Lamp Base |
| 1545 | The Old Woman who Lived in a Shoe |
| 1675 | Goody Tiptoes |
| 1676/1 | Tabitha Twitchet (First Version) |
| 1676/2 | Tabitha Twitchet (Second Version) |
| 1796 | Old Mr. Brown |
| 1851 | Anna Maria |
| 1940/1 | Mr. Benjamin Bunny (First Version) |
| 1940/2 | Mr. Benjamin Bunny (Second Version) |
| 1941/1 | Cecily Parsley (First Version) |
| 1941/2 | Cecily Parsley (Second Version) |
| 1942 | Mrs. Flopsy Bunny |
| 2061 | Amiable Guinea Pig |
| 2082 | Jemima Puddle-Duck Plaque |
| 2083 | Peter Rabbit Plaque (First Version) |
| 2085 | Tom Kitten Plaque |
| 2276 | Aunt Pettitoes |
| 2284 | Cousin Ribby |
| 2295 | Display Stand |
| 2333/1 | Appley Dapply (First Version) |
| 2333/2 | Appley Dapply (Second Version) |
| 2334 | Pickles |
| 2381 | Pig-Wig |
| 2424 | Mr. Alderman Ptoleme |
| 2425 | Sir Isaac Newton |
| 2452/1 | Sally Henny Penny (First Version) |
| 2452/2 | Sally Henny Penny (Second Version) |
| 2453/1 | Mr. Jackson (First Version) |
| 2453/2 | Mr. Jackson (Second Version) |
| 2508 | Simpkin |
| 2509 | Mr. Benjamin Bunny and Peter Rabbit |
| 2543 | Mrs. Rabbit and Bunnies |
| 2544 | Tabitha Twitchet and Miss Moppet |
| 2559 | Ginger |
| 2560 | Poorly Peter Rabbit |
| 2584 | Hunca Munca Sweeping |
| 2585 | Little Black Rabbit |
| 2586/1 | Fierce Bad Rabbit (First Version) |
| 2586/2 | Fierce BadRabbit (Second Version) |
| 2594 | Jemima Puddle-Duck and Foxy Whiskered Gentleman Plaque |
| 2601 | Duchess (Style Two) |
| 2627 | Chippy Hackee |
| 2628 | Mr. Drake Puddle-Duck |
| 2647 | Rebeccah Puddle-Duck |
| 2650 | Peter Rabbit Plaque (Second Version) |
| 2668 | Thomasina Tittlemouse |
| 2685 | Mrs. Tittlemouse Plaque |
| 2713 | Diggory Diggory Delvet |
| 2716 | Susan |
| 2767 | Old Mr. Pricklepin |
| 2803/1 | Benjamin Bunny Sat on a Bank |
| 2803/2 | Benjamin Bunny Sat on a Bank |
| 2804 | The Old Woman who Lived in a Shoe Knitting |
| 2823 | Jemima Puddle-Duck Made a Feather Nest |
| 2877 | Mrs. Tiggy-Winkle Takes Tea |
| 2878 | Cottontail |
| 2956 | Old Mr. Bouncer |
| 2957 | Goody and Timmy Tiptoes |
| 2965 | John Joiner |
| 2966 | Mother Ladybird |
| 2971 | Babbitty Bumble |
| 2989 | Tom Thumb |
| 2996 | Timmy Willie Sleeping |
| 3030 | Tom Kitten and Butterfly |
| 3031 | Little Pig Robinson Spying |
| 3090 | Mr. Jeremy Fisher Digging |
| 3091 | Mr. Tod |
| 3094 | Johnny Town-Mouse with Bag |
| 3157 | Peter Rabbit in the Gooseberry Net |
| 3193 | Jemima Puddle-Duck and Foxy Whiskered Gentleman |
| 3197 | Mittens and Moppet |
| 3200 | Gentleman Mouse Made a Bow |
| 3219 | Foxy Reading Country News |
| 3220 | Lady Mouse Made a Curtsey |
| 3234 | Benjamin Wakes Up |
| 3242 | Peter and the Red Pocket Handkerchief |
| 3251 | Miss Dormouse |
| 3252 | Pigling Eats his Porridge |
| 3257 | Christmas Stocking |
| 3278 | Mrs. Rabbit Cooking |
| 3288 | Hunca Munca Spills the Beads |
| 3317 | Benjamin Ate a Lettuce Leaf |
| 3319 | And This Pig Had None |
| 3325 | No More Twist |
| | Jemima Puddle-Duck Character Jug |
| | Mr. Jeremy Fisher Character Jug |
| 3102 | Mrs. Tiggy-Winkle Character Jug |
| 2959 | Old Mr. Brown Character Jug |
| | Peter Rabbit Character Jug |
| | Tom Kitten Character Jug |

## *NUMERICAL INDEX TO DOULTON BRAMBLEY HEDGE FIGURINES*

| | |
|---|---|
| DBH1 | Poppy Eyebright |
| DBH2 | Mr. Apple |
| DBH3 | Mrs. Apple |
| DBH4 | Lord Woodhouse |
| DBH5 | Lady Woodmouse |
| DBH6 | Dusty Dogwood |
| DBH7 | Wilfrid Toadflax |
| DBH8 | Primrose Woodmouse |
| DBH9 | Old Mrs. Eyebright |
| DBH10 | Mr. Toadflax |
| DBH11 | Mrs. Toadflax |
| DBH12 | Catkin |
| DBH13 | Old Vole |
| DBH14 | Basil |
| DBH15 | Mrs. Crustybread |
| DBH16 | Clover |
| DBH17 | Teasel |
| DBH18 | Store Stump Money Box |

| | |
|---|---|
| DBH19 | Lily Weaver |
| DBH20 | Flax Weaver |
| DBH21 | Conker |
| DBH22 | Primrose Entertains |
| DBH23 | Wilfrid Entertains |
| DBH24 | Mr. Saltapple |
| DBH25 | Mrs. Saltapple |

## *NUMERICAL INDEX TO ROYAL DOULTON BUNNYKINS FIGURINES*

| | |
|---|---|
| D6001 | Billy Bunnykins |
| D6002 | Mary Bunnykins |
| D6003 | Farmer Bunnykins |
| D6004 | Mother Bunnykins |
| D6024 | Freddie Bunnykins |
| D6025 | Reggie Bunnykins |
| DB1 | Family Photograph Bunnykins (First Version) |
| DB2 | Buntie Bunnykins Helping Mother |
| DB3 | Billie Bunnykins Cooling Off |
| DB4 | Billie And Buntie Bunnykins Sleigh Ride (First Version) |
| DB5 | Mr. Bunnykins Autumn Days |
| DB6 | Mrs. Bunnykins Clean Sweep |
| DB7 | Daisie Bunnykins Springtime |
| DB8 | Dollie Bunnykins Playtime (First Version) |
| DB9 | Storytime (First Version) |
| DB10 | Busy Needles Bunnykins |
| DB11 | Rise And Shine Bunnykins |
| DB12 | Tally Ho! Bunnykins (First Version) |
| DB13 | The Artist |
| DB14 | Grandpa's Story Bunnykins |
| DB15 | Sleepytime |
| DB16 | Mr. Bunnybeat Strumming |
| DB17 | Santa Bunnykins Happy Christmas |
| DB18 | Mr. Bunnykins At The Easter Parade (First Version) |
| DB19 | Mrs. Bunnykins At The Easter Parade (First Version) |
| DB20 | Astro Bunnykins Rocket Man |
| DB21 | Happy Birthday Bunnykins |
| DB22 | Jogging Bunnykins |
| DB23 | Sousaphone Bunnykins (First Version) |
| DB24 | Trumpeter Bunnykins (First Version) |
| DB25 | Cymbals Bunnykins (First Version) |
| DB26 | Drummer Bunnykins Bunnykins, Oompah Band Edition (First Version) |
| DB26b | Drummer Bunnykins 50th Anniversary Edition (Second Version) |
| DB27 | Drum-major Bunnykins (First Version) |
| DB28a | Olympic Bunnykins (First Version) |
| DB28b | Olympic Bunnykins (Second Version) |
| DB29a | Touchdown Bunnykins (First Version) |
| DB29b | Touchdown Bunnykins (Second Version) |
| DB30 | Knockout Bunnykins |
| DB31 | Downhill Bunnykins |
| DB32 | Bogey Bunnykins |
| DB33a | Tally Ho! Music Box (First Version) |
| DB33b | Tally Ho! Music Box (Second Version) |
| DB34 | Santa Bunnykins Music Box |
| DB35 | Astro Bunnykins Rocket Man Music Box |
| DB36 | Happy Birthday Bunnykins Music Box |
| DB37 | Jogging Bunnykins Music Box |
| DB38 | Mr. Bunnybeat Strumming Music Box |
| DB39 | Mrs. Bunnykins At The East Parade Music Box |
| DB40 | Aerobic Bunnykins |
| DB41 | Freefall Bunnykins |
| DB42 | Ace Bunnykins |
| DB43 | Home Run Bunnykins (1 On Back Of Jersey) |
| DB45 | King John (First Version) |
| DB46 | Queen Sophie (First Version) |
| DB47 | Princess Beatrice (First Version) |
| DB48 | Prince Frederick (First Version) |
| DB49 | Harry The Herald (First Version) |
| DB50 | Uncle Sam Bunnykins |
| DB51 | Mr. Bunnykins At The Easter Parade (Second Version) |
| DB52 | Mrs. Bunnykins At The Easter Parade (Second Version) |
| DB53 | Carol Singer Music Box |
| DB54 | Collector Bunnykins |
| DB55 | Bedtime Bunnykins (First Version) |
| DB56 | Be Prepared Bunnykins |
| DB57 | School Days Bunnykins |
| DB58 | Australian Bunnykins |
| DB59 | Storytime Bunnykins (Second Version) |
| DB60 | Schoolmaster Bunnykins |
| DB61 | Brownie Bunnykins |
| DB62 | Santa Bunnykins Happy Christmas, Christmas Tree Ornament |
| DB63 | Bedtime Bunnykins (Second Version) |
| DB64 | Policeman Bunnykins |
| DB65 | Lollipopman Bunnykins |
| DB66 | Schoolboy Bunnykins |
| DB67 | Family Photograph (Second Version) |
| DB68 | Father, Mother And Victoria Bunnykins |
| DB69 | William Bunnykins |
| DB70 | Susan Bunnykins |
| DB71 | Polly Bunnykins |
| DB72 | Tom Bunnykins |
| DB73 | Harry Bunnykins |
| DB74a | Nurse Bunnykins (First Version) |
| DB74b | Nurse Bunnykins (Second Version) |
| DB75 | Fireman Bunnykins |
| DB76 | Postman Bunnykins |
| DB77 | Paperboy Bunnykins |
| DB78 | Tally Ho! Bunnykins (Second Version) |
| DB79 | Bedtime Bunnykins (Third Version) |
| DB80 | Dollie Bunnykins Playtime (Second Version) |
| DB81 | Billie & Buntie Bunnykins Sleigh Ride (Second Version) |
| DB82 | Ice Cream Bunnykins |
| DB83 | Susan Bunnykins As Queen Of The May |
| DB84 | Fisherman Bunnykins |
| DB85 | Cook Bunnykins |
| DB86 | Sousaphone Bunnykins From The Oompah Band (Second Version) |

| | |
|---|---|
| DB87 | Trumpeter Bunnykins From The Oompah Band (Second Version) |
| DB88 | Cymbals Bunnykins From The Oompah Band (Second Version) |
| DB89 | Drummer Bunnykins (Third Version) |
| DB90 | Drum-major Bunnykins (Second Version) |
| DB91 | King John (Second Version) |
| DB92 | Queen Sophie (Second Version) |
| DB93 | Princess Beatrice (Second Version) |
| DB94 | Prince Frederick (Second Version) |
| DB95 | Harry The Herald (Second Version ) |
| DB96 | Touchdown Bunnykins Ohio State University (Third Version) |
| DB97 | Touchdown Bunnykins University Of Michigan (Fourth Version) |
| DB98 | Touchdown Bunnykins Cincinnati Bengals (Fifth Version) |
| DB99 | Touchdown Bunnykins Notre Dame College (Sixth Version) |
| DB100 | Touchdown Bunnykins University Of Indiana (Seventh Version) |
| DB101 | Bride Bunnykins |
| DB102 | Groom Bunnykins |
| DB103 | Bedtime Bunnykins (Fourth Version) |
| DB104 | Carol Singer Bunnykins |
| DB105 | Sousaphone Bunnykins From The Oompah Band (Third Version) |
| DB106 | Trumpeter Bunnykins From The Oompah Band (Third Version) |
| DB107 | Cymbals Bunnykins From The Oompah Band (Third Version) |
| DB108 | Drummer Bunnykins (Fourth Version) |
| DB109 | Drum-major Bunnykins From The Oompah Band (Third Version) |
| DB115 | Harry The Herald (Third Version) |
| DB116 | Goalkeeper Bunnykins (First Version ) |
| DB117 | Footballer Bunnykins (First Version) |
| DB118 | Goalkeeper Bunnykins (Second Version) |
| DB119 | Footballer Bunnykins (Second Version) |
| DB120 | Goalkeeper Bunnykins (Third Version) |
| DB121 | Footballer Bunnykins (Third Version) |
| DB122 | Goalkeeper Bunnykins (Fourth Version) |
| DB123 | Soccer Player Bunnykins |
| DB124 | Rock 'n' Roll Bunnykins |
| DB125 | Milkman Bunnykins |
| DB126 | Magician Bunnykins |
| DB127 | Guardsman Bunnykins |
| DB128 | Clown Bunnykins (First Version) |
| DB129 | Clown Bunnykins (Second Version) |
| DB130 | Sweetheart Bunnykins |
| DB131 | Master Potter Bunnykins |
| DB132 | Halloween Bunnykins |
| DB133 | Aussie Surfer Bunnykins |
| DB134 | John Bull Bunnykins |
| DB135 | Constable Mountie Bunnykins |
| DB136 | Sergeant Mountie Bunnykins |
| DB137 | 60th Anniversary Bunnykins |
| DB142 | Cheerleader Bunnykins |
| DB143 | Cheerleader Bunnykins |
| DB144 | Batsman Bunnykins |
| DB145 | Bowler Bunnykins |
| DB146 | Christmas Surprise Bunnykins |
| DB147 | Rainy Day Bunnykins |
| DB148 | Bathtime Bunnykins |
| DB149 | Easter Greeting Bunnykins |
| DB150 | Wicket Keeper Bunnykins |
| D6615a | Bunny Bank (First Version) |
| D6615b | Bunny Bank (Second Version) |
| | City Gent Tea Pot |

## *NUMERICAL INDEX TO ROYAL DOULTON SNOWMEN FIGURES*

| | |
|---|---|
| DS1 | James |
| DS2 | The Snowman |
| DS3 | Stylish Snowman |
| DS4 | Thank You Snowman |
| DS5 | Snowman Magic - Music Box |
| DS6 | Cowboy Snowman |
| DS7 | Highland Snowman |
| DS8 | Lady Snowman |
| DS9 | Bass Drummer Snowman |
| DS10 | Flautist Snowman |
| DS11 | Violinist Snowman |
| DS12 | Pianist Snowman |
| DS13 | Snowman's Piano |
| DS14 | Cymbal Player Snowman |
| DS15 | Drummer Snowman |
| DS16 | Trumpeter Snowman |
| DS17 | Cellist Snowman |
| DS18 | Snowman Musical Box |
| DS19 | Snowman Money Box |
| DS20 | The Snowman Tobogganing |
| DS21 | The Snowman Skiing |
| DS22 | The Snowballing Snowman |
| DS23 | Building The Snowman |
| D6972 | Snowman Miniature Character Jug |

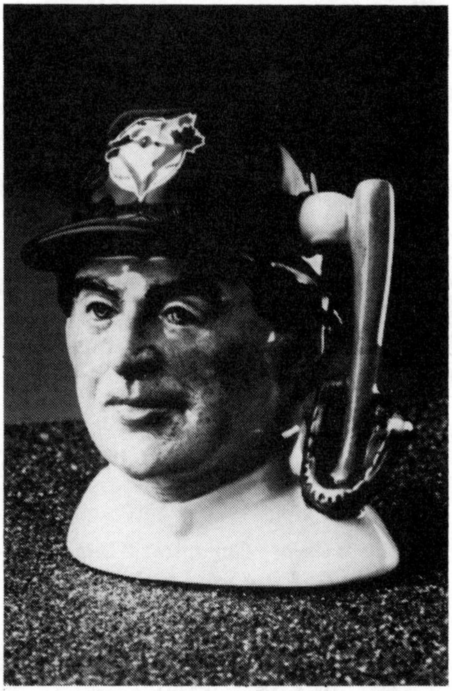

# THE AUTHORITIES!

*For Reference & Pricing Nothing Surpasses*

*The Charlton Catalogues...*

### *THE CHARLTON STANDARD CATALOGUE of ROYAL DOULTON FIGURINES*
### *— 4th Edition —*

**The world's most popular and comprehensive Doulton figurine pricing catalogue! Complete HN and M Series are illustrated & priced in Canadian, U.S. dollars and in British pounds. Over 2,000 figurines are arranged in HN order and listed with name, designer, height, colour, date of manufacture and varieties. Including an introduction by Doulton historian Louise Irvine. Complete alphabetical index for easy checking and cross reference. Over 400 pages!**

### *THE CHARLTON PRICE GUIDE of ROYAL DOULTON ANIMALS*
### *— First Edition —*

**This eagerly-awaited pricing reference lists, illustrates and prices the Royal Doulton Animal Figures. All HN, K and DA numbers are included as are the flambé and Chinese Jade animals. Current market prices are given in Canadian and U.S. currencies as well as British pounds. The catalogue highlights model number, size, colour, designer, dates of manufacture in addition to discontinued dates and varieties. The book has more than 1,200 photos plus an introduction by Doulton Historian Louise Irvine. Features an easy to use alphabetical index. The most authoritative reference on the subject today. Over 450 pages!**

***Available at Fine Collectable Shops or directly from the Publisher.***

*The Charlton Press*

**2010 Yonge Street, Toronto, Ontario M4S 1Z9 416-488-4653 Fax 416-488-4656**